GRILLING

Publications International, Ltd.

Front cover photograph © Shutterstock.com

Pictured on the back cover *(left to right):* Beer and Orange Marinated Tuna Steaks *(page 128),* Backyard Barbecue Burgers *(page 56)* and Mexican-Style Corn on the Cob *(page 172).*

ISBN: 978-1-68022-284-5

Library of Congress Control Number: 2015951032

Manufactured in China.

8 7 6 5 4 3 2 1

Microwave Cooking: Microwave ovens vary in wattage. Use the cooking times as guidelines and check for doneness before adding more time.

TABLE OF CONTENTS

⭐

APPETIZERS

GRILLED SALMON QUESADILLAS
WITH CUCUMBER SALSA
MAKES 4 SERVINGS

1 medium cucumber, peeled, seeded and finely chopped

½ cup green or red salsa

1 salmon fillet (8 ounces)

3 tablespoons olive oil, divided

4 (10-inch) flour tortillas, warmed

6 ounces goat cheese, crumbled *or* 1½ cups (6 ounces) shredded Monterey Jack cheese

¼ cup pickled jalapeño slices, drained

1 Prepare grill for direct cooking.

2 Combine cucumber and salsa in small bowl; set aside. Brush salmon with 2 tablespoons oil.

3 Grill salmon, covered, over medium-high heat 5 to 6 minutes per side or until fish begins to flake when tested with fork. Transfer to plate; flake with fork.

4 Spread salmon evenly over half of each tortilla, leaving 1-inch border. Sprinkle with goat cheese and jalapeño slices. Fold tortillas in half; brush with remaining 1 tablespoon oil.

5 Grill quesadillas over medium-high heat until browned on both sides and cheese is melted. Cut into wedges; serve with salsa.

MARINATED BEEF BROCHETTES
MAKES 6 SERVINGS

12 ounces beef tenderloin, cut into 1-inch pieces

¼ cup finely chopped onion

¼ cup olive oil

3 tablespoons lime juice

1 finely chopped seeded hot finger pepper (about 1 teaspoon)

1 clove garlic, minced

1 medium green bell pepper, cut into 1-inch pieces

1 medium red onion, cut into 1-inch pieces

1 Place beef in large resealable food storage bag. Combine chopped onion, oil, lime juice, hot pepper and garlic in medium bowl; pour over beef. Seal bag; turn to coat. Marinate in refrigerator 2 hours or overnight.

2 Soak six 8-inch wooden skewers in water 20 minutes. Prepare grill for direct cooking.

3 Remove beef from marinade; discard marinade. Alternately thread beef, bell pepper and red onion onto skewers.

4 Grill brochettes over medium-high heat 2 to 3 minutes per side or to desired doneness.

MOJITO SHRIMP COCKTAIL
MAKES 6 TO 8 SERVINGS

1 pound frozen medium raw shrimp, unpeeled and deveined (with tails on)
1 cup plus 2 tablespoons prepared mojito cocktail mix, divided
2 tablespoons olive oil
1 jar shrimp cocktail sauce
    Lime wedges (optional)

1 Place shrimp in large shallow glass dish; separate shrimp as much as possible to aid thawing. Pour 1 cup mojito mix over shrimp; cover and marinate in refrigerator 10 to 24 hours or until thawed, stirring once or twice.

2 Prepare grill for direct cooking. Drain shrimp; discard marinade. *Do not peel shrimp.* Pat dry and place in large bowl with oil; toss to coat.

3 Grill shrimp on grill topper over medium-high heat 10 to 12 minutes or until shrimp are pink and opaque, turning once. Refrigerate until ready to serve.

4 Pour cocktail sauce into serving bowl; stir in remaining 2 tablespoons mojito mix. Peel shrimp before serving or provide bowl for shells. Serve with lime wedges, if desired.

• • • • • • • • • • • • • • • • • • •

TIP
For extra flavor, add chopped fresh mint to the cocktail sauce along with the mojito mix.

GRILLED FETA WITH PEPPERS
MAKES 8 SERVINGS

¼ cup thinly sliced sweet onion

1 package (8 ounces) feta cheese, cut in half horizontally

¼ cup thinly sliced green bell pepper

¼ cup thinly sliced red bell pepper

½ teaspoon dried oregano

¼ teaspoon garlic pepper or black pepper

24 (½-inch) slices French bread

1 Prepare grill for direct cooking.

2 Spray 14-inch-long sheet of foil with nonstick cooking spray. Place onion in center of foil; top with feta. Sprinkle with bell peppers, oregano and garlic pepper. Seal foil using Drugstore Wrap technique (see below).

3 Place foil packet upside down on grid. Grill, covered, over high heat 15 minutes. Turn packet and grill 15 minutes.

4 Open packet carefully; serve immediately with bread.

DRUGSTORE WRAP

Place the food in the center of an oblong piece of heavy-duty foil, leaving at least a 2-inch border around the food. Bring two long sides together above the food; fold down in a series of locked folds, allowing for heat circulation and expansion. Fold the short ends up and over again. Press the folds firmly to seal the foil packet.

THAI COFFEE CHICKEN SKEWERS
MAKES 8 SKEWERS

1¼ pounds chicken tenders

⅓ cup soy sauce

¼ cup strong brewed coffee

2 tablespoons plus 2 teaspoons lime juice, divided

4 cloves garlic, minced, divided

1 tablespoon plus 1 teaspoon grated fresh ginger, divided

½ teaspoon sriracha or hot chili sauce, divided

¼ cup hoisin sauce

2 tablespoons creamy peanut butter

1 tablespoon tomato paste

1 teaspoon sugar

½ cup water

4 green onions, cut into 1-inch pieces

1 Cut chicken crosswise into ½-inch-wide strips; place in large resealable food storage bag. Combine soy sauce, coffee, 2 tablespoons lime juice, 2 cloves garlic, 1 teaspoon ginger and ¼ teaspoon sriracha in small bowl; pour over chicken. Seal bag; turn to coat. Marinate in refrigerator 1 to 2 hours.

2 Soak eight 12-inch wooden skewers in water 20 minutes. Prepare grill for direct cooking.

3 Combine hoisin sauce, peanut butter, tomato paste, sugar, water, remaining 1 tablespoon ginger, 2 cloves garlic, 2 teaspoons lime juice and ¼ teaspoon sriracha sauce in medium bowl; mix well.

4 Remove chicken from marinade; discard marinade. Alternately thread chicken and green onions onto skewers.

5 Grill skewers over medium heat 6 to 8 minutes or until chicken is cooked through, turning once. Serve with peanut sauce.

PARMESAN POLENTA
MAKES 6 SERVINGS

4 cups vegetable or chicken broth

1 small onion, minced

4 cloves garlic, minced

1 tablespoon minced fresh rosemary *or* 1 teaspoon dried rosemary

½ teaspoon salt

1¼ cups yellow cornmeal

6 tablespoons grated Parmesan cheese

1 tablespoon olive oil, divided

1 Spray 11×7-inch baking pan with nonstick cooking spray. Spray one side of 7-inch-long sheet of waxed paper with cooking spray.

2 Combine broth, onion, garlic, rosemary and salt in medium saucepan; bring to a boil over high heat. Gradually add cornmeal, stirring constantly. Reduce heat to medium; simmer 30 minutes or until mixture has consistency of thick mashed potatoes. Remove from heat; stir in Parmesan.

3 Spread polenta evenly in prepared pan; place waxed paper, sprayed side down, on polenta and smooth surface. (If surface is bumpy, it is more likely to stick to grill.) Cool on wire rack 15 minutes or until firm. Remove waxed paper; cut into six squares and remove from pan.

4 Prepare grill for direct cooking. Oil grid. Brush tops of polenta squares with half of oil.

5 Grill polenta, oil side down, covered, over low to medium heat 6 to 8 minutes or until golden brown. Brush with remaining oil; turn and grill 6 to 8 minutes or until golden brown. Serve warm.

SWEET AND SOUR SHRIMP SKEWERS
MAKES 10 TO 12 SERVINGS

8 ounces medium raw shrimp, peeled and deveined (with tails on)

1 can (8 ounces) pineapple chunks in juice, drained

¼ cup sweet and sour sauce, plus additional for serving

1 Soak wooden skewers in water 20 minutes. Prepare grill for direct cooking.

2 Alternately thread shrimp and pineapple onto skewers. Brush with ¼ cup sweet and sour sauce.

3 Grill skewers over medium-high heat 3 minutes per side or until shrimp are pink and opaque. Serve with additional sweet and sour sauce for dipping, if desired.

GRILLED VIETNAMESE-STYLE CHICKEN WINGS
MAKES 6 TO 8 SERVINGS

3 pounds chicken wings

⅓ cup honey

¼ to ½ cup sliced lemongrass

¼ cup fish sauce

2 tablespoons chopped garlic

2 tablespoons chopped shallots

2 tablespoons chopped fresh ginger

2 tablespoons lime juice

2 tablespoons canola oil

Chopped fresh cilantro (optional)

1 Remove and discard wing tips. Cut each wing in half at joint. Place wings in large resealable food storage bag.

2 Combine honey, lemongrass, fish sauce, garlic, shallots, ginger, lime juice and oil in food processor; process until smooth. Pour over wings. Seal bag; turn to coat. Marinate in refrigerator 4 hours or overnight.

3 Prepare grill for direct cooking. Preheat oven to 350°F. Remove wings from marinade; reserve marinade.

4 Grill wings over medium heat 10 minutes or until browned, turning and basting occasionally with marinade. Discard any remaining marinade.

5 Arrange wings in single layer on baking sheet. Bake 20 minutes or until cooked through. Sprinkle with cilantro, if desired.

GRILLED LOBSTER, SHRIMP AND CALAMARI CEVICHE
MAKES 6 SERVINGS

¾ cup orange juice

⅓ cup lime juice

2 jalapeño peppers,* seeded and minced

2 tablespoons chopped fresh cilantro, chives or green onion tops

2 tablespoons tequila

1 teaspoon honey

1 teaspoon ground cumin

1 teaspoon olive oil

10 squid, cleaned and cut into rings and tentacles

½ pound medium raw shrimp, peeled and deveined

2 lobster tails (8 ounces each), meat removed and shells discarded

Jalapeño peppers can sting and irritate the skin, so wear rubber gloves when handling peppers and do not touch your eyes.

1 Combine orange juice, lime juice, jalapeños, cilantro, tequila and honey in large bowl; mix well. Measure ¼ cup marinade into small bowl; stir in cumin and oil. Set aside for shrimp and lobster. Refrigerate remaining marinade.

2 Prepare grill for direct cooking.

3 Bring 1 quart water to a boil in large saucepan over high heat. Add squid; cook 30 seconds or until opaque. Drain and rinse under cold water. Add squid to refrigerated marinade.

4 Thread shrimp onto metal skewers. Brush shrimp and lobster with reserved ¼ cup marinade.

5 Grill shrimp over medium-high heat 2 to 3 minutes per side or until pink and opaque. Remove shrimp from skewers; add to squid.

6 Grill lobster 5 minutes per side or until meat is opaque and cooked through. Cut lobster meat into ¼-inch-thick slices; add to squid and shrimp mixture. Cover and refrigerate at least 2 hours or overnight.

SPICED CHICKEN SKEWERS WITH YOGURT-TAHINI SAUCE
MAKES 8 SERVINGS

1 cup plain Greek yogurt

¼ cup chopped fresh parsley, plus additional for garnish

¼ cup tahini

2 tablespoons lemon juice

1 clove garlic

¾ teaspoon salt, divided

1 tablespoon vegetable oil

2 teaspoons garam masala*

1 pound boneless skinless chicken breasts, cut into 1-inch pieces

Garam masala is a blend of Indian spices available in the spice aisle of many supermarkets. If garam masala is unavailable, substitute 1 teaspoon each ground cumin and ground coriander.

1 Soak eight 6-inch wooden skewers in water 20 minutes. Prepare grill for direct cooking. Oil grid.

2 Combine yogurt, ¼ cup parsley, tahini, lemon juice, garlic and ¼ teaspoon salt in food processor or blender; process until well blended.

3 Combine oil, garam masala and remaining ½ teaspoon salt in medium bowl. Add chicken; toss to coat. Thread chicken onto skewers.

4 Grill skewers over medium-high heat 5 minutes per side or until chicken is cooked through. Serve with sauce; garnish with additional parsley.

BEEF

STEAK PARMESAN
MAKES 2 TO 3 SERVINGS

4 cloves garlic, minced

1 tablespoon olive oil

1 tablespoon coarse salt

1 teaspoon dried rosemary

1 teaspoon black pepper

2 beef T-bone or Porterhouse steaks, 1 inch thick (about 2 pounds)

¼ cup grated Parmesan cheese

1 Prepare grill for direct cooking.

2 Combine garlic, oil, salt, rosemary and pepper in small bowl; spread over both sides of steaks. Let stand 15 minutes.

3 Grill steaks, covered, over medium-high heat 14 to 19 minutes for medium rare (145°F), turning once. Transfer to cutting board; sprinkle with Parmesan. Tent with foil; let stand 10 minutes before serving.

TIP

For a smoky flavor, soak 2 cups hickory or oak wood chips in cold water to cover at least 30 minutes. Drain and scatter over hot coals before grilling.

STEAK AND MUSHROOM SKEWERS
MAKES 4 SERVINGS

¼ cup Italian vinaigrette

2 tablespoons Worcestershire sauce

12 ounces beef top sirloin steak, cut into 24 (1-inch) cubes

24 medium whole mushrooms (about 12 ounces)

¼ cup mayonnaise

¼ cup sour cream

1 clove garlic, minced

¼ to ½ teaspoon dried rosemary

¼ teaspoon salt

1 medium zucchini, cut into 24 (1-inch) pieces

1 medium green bell pepper, cut into 24 (1-inch) pieces

1 Combine vinaigrette and Worcestershire sauce in small bowl; mix well. Reserve 2 tablespoons dressing mixture. Combine beef, mushrooms and remaining vinaigrette mixture in large resealable food storage bag. Seal bag; turn to coat. Marinate in refrigerator 30 to 60 minutes.

2 Combine mayonnaise, sour cream, garlic, rosemary and salt in medium bowl; mix well. Cover and refrigerate until ready to serve.

3 Soak eight 10-inch wooden skewers in water 20 minutes. Prepare grill for direct cooking.

4 Alternately thread beef, mushrooms, zucchini and bell pepper onto skewers. Discard remaining marinade.

5 Grill skewers over medium-high heat 6 to 8 minutes or to desired doneness, turning occasionally. Before serving, brush with reserved 2 tablespoons dressing mixture. Serve with sauce.

SPICY SMOKED BEEF RIBS
MAKES 4 TO 6 SERVINGS

4 wood pieces for smoking

4 to 6 pounds beef back ribs, cut into 3- to 4-rib portions

Black pepper

1⅓ cups barbecue sauce

2 teaspoons hot pepper sauce or Szechuan chili sauce

Beer, at room temperature, or hot water

1 Soak wood pieces in water at least 30 minutes; drain.

2 Spread ribs on large baking sheet; season with black pepper. Combine barbecue sauce and hot pepper sauce in small bowl; mix well. Brush ribs with half of sauce. Marinate in refrigerator 30 minutes to 1 hour.

3 Prepare grill for indirect cooking. Add soaked wood to fire; place foil drip pan in center of grill. Fill pan half full with beer.

4 Place ribs on grid, meaty side up, directly above drip pan. Grill ribs, covered, over low heat about 1 hour or until meat is tender, brushing remaining sauce over ribs 2 or 3 times during cooking. (If grill has thermometer, maintain cooking temperature at 250°F to 275°F.) Add additional soaked wood after 30 minutes, if necessary.

GRILLED STRIP STEAKS WITH CHIMICHURRI

MAKES 4 SERVINGS

Chimichurri (recipe follows)

4 strip steaks (8 ounces each, about 1 inch thick)

¾ teaspoon salt

¾ teaspoon ground cumin

¼ teaspoon black pepper

1 Prepare grill for direct cooking. Oil grid. Prepare Chimichurri. Sprinkle both sides of steaks with salt, cumin and pepper.

2 Grill steaks, covered, over medium-high heat 4 to 5 minutes per side for medium rare (145°F) or to desired doneness. Serve with Chimichurri.

CHIMICHURRI

MAKES ABOUT 1 CUP

½ cup packed fresh basil leaves

⅓ cup extra virgin olive oil

¼ cup packed fresh parsley

2 tablespoons packed fresh cilantro leaves

2 tablespoons lemon juice

1 clove garlic

½ teaspoon salt

½ teaspoon grated orange peel

¼ teaspoon ground coriander

⅛ teaspoon black pepper

Combine all ingredients in food processor or blender; process until blended.

BACON AND BLUE CHEESE STUFFED BURGERS
MAKES 4 SERVINGS

4 slices applewood-smoked bacon or regular bacon

1 small red onion, finely chopped

2 tablespoons crumbled blue cheese

1 tablespoon butter, softened

1½ pounds ground beef

Salt and black pepper

4 onion or plain hamburger rolls

Lettuce leaves

1 Cook bacon in large skillet over medium-high heat until almost crisp. Drain on paper towel-lined plate. Finely chop bacon; place in small bowl. Add onion to same skillet; cook and stir 5 minutes or until softened. Add to bowl with bacon. Cool slightly; stir in blue cheese and butter until well blended.

2 Prepare grill for direct cooking.

3 Divide beef into eight portions. Flatten into thin patties about 4 inches wide; season with salt and pepper. Place 2 tablespoons bacon mixture in center of each of four patties; cover with remaining patties. Pinch edges together to seal.

4 Grill patties, covered, over medium-high heat 4 to 5 minutes per side until cooked through (160°F) or to desired doneness. Serve burgers on rolls with lettuce.

GRILLED SKIRT STEAK FAJITAS
MAKES 4 SERVINGS

1½ pounds skirt steak

½ cup pale ale

3 tablespoons lime juice

1 teaspoon ground cumin

2 tablespoons olive oil

1 cup thinly sliced red onion

1 cup thinly sliced red and green bell peppers

2 cloves garlic, minced

3 plum tomatoes, each cut into 4 wedges

1 tablespoon reduced-sodium soy sauce

¾ teaspoon salt

¼ teaspoon black pepper

8 (7-inch) flour tortillas, warmed

Lime wedges and salsa (optional)

1 Place steak in large resealable food storage bag. Combine ale, lime juice and cumin in small bowl; pour over steak. Seal bag; turn to coat. Marinate in refrigerator 2 hours, turning occasionally.

2 Heat oil in large nonstick skillet over medium-high heat. Add onion; cook and stir 2 to 3 minutes or until beginning to soften. Add bell peppers; cook and stir 7 to 8 minutes or until softened. Add garlic; cook and stir 1 minute. Add tomatoes; cook 2 minutes or just until tomatoes begin to soften. Add soy sauce; cook 1 minute. Keep warm.

3 Prepare grill for direct cooking. Oil grid. Remove steak from marinade; discard marinade. Sprinkle with salt and black pepper.

4 Grill steak over medium-high heat 4 to 6 minutes per side for medium rare (145°F) or to desired doneness. Transfer to cutting board. Tent with foil; let stand 10 minutes before slicing.

5 Cut steak across the grain into ¼-inch-thick slices. Fill tortillas with steak and vegetable mixture; serve with lime wedges and salsa, if desired.

GREEK-STYLE STEAK SANDWICHES
MAKES 8 SANDWICHES

2 teaspoons Greek seasoning or dried oregano

1 beef flank steak (about 1½ pounds)

4 pita bread rounds, sliced in half crosswise

1 small cucumber, thinly sliced

½ cup sliced red onion

½ cup chopped tomato

½ cup crumbled feta cheese

¼ cup red wine vinaigrette

1 cup plain yogurt

1 Rub Greek seasoning over both sides of steak. Place on plate; cover and refrigerate 30 to 60 minutes.

2 Prepare grill for direct cooking.

3 Grill steak, covered, over medium-high heat 17 to 21 minutes for medium rare (145°F) or to desired doneness, turning once. Transfer to cutting board. Tent with foil; let stand 10 minutes before slicing.

4 Meanwhile, grill pita halves about 1 minute per side or until warm. Slice steak against the grain into thin strips; divide evnly among pita halves. Top with cucumber, onion, tomato and feta; drizzle with vinaigrette. Serve with yogurt.

BEEF AND BLUEBERRY SALAD
MAKES 4 SERVINGS

1¼ pounds boneless beef sirloin steak, 1 inch thick

½ cup reduced-sodium teriyaki sauce

¼ cup orange juice

¼ teaspoon hot pepper sauce

8 cups sliced napa cabbage or bok choy

2 cups fresh blueberries

½ cup fresh raspberries

½ cup raspberry vinaigrette

1 Place steak in large resealable food storage bag. Combine teriyaki sauce, orange juice and hot pepper sauce in small bowl; pour over steak. Seal bag; turn to coat. Marinate in refrigerator at least 4 hours or up to 24 hours, turning occasionally.

2 Prepare grill for direct cooking. Drain steak; discard marinade.

3 Grill steak over medium heat 4 to 6 minutes per side for medium rare (145°F), 6 to 8 minutes per side for medium (160°F) or to desired doneness, turning once. Transfer to cutting board. Tent with foil; let stand 10 minutes before slicing.

4 Cut steak into very thin strips. Combine cabbage, blueberries, raspberries and steak in large bowl. Drizzle with vinaigrette; toss gently to coat.

BEEF SPIEDINI WITH ORZO
MAKES 4 SERVINGS

1½ pounds beef top sirloin steak, cut into 1×1¼-inch pieces

¼ cup olive oil

¼ cup dry red wine

2 cloves garlic, minced

1 teaspoon dried rosemary

1 teaspoon salt, divided

½ teaspoon dried thyme

½ teaspoon coarsely ground black pepper

6 cups water

1 cup uncooked orzo pasta

1 tablespoon butter

1 tablespoon chopped fresh parsley

Fresh rosemary sprigs (optional)

1 Place beef in large resealable food storage bag. Combine oil, wine, garlic, dried rosemary, ½ teaspoon salt, thyme and pepper in small bowl; pour over beef. Seal bag; turn to coat. Marinate in refrigerator 15 to 30 minutes.

2 Soak eight 6- to 8-inch wooden skewers in water 20 minutes. (See Tip.) Prepare grill for direct cooking.

3 Bring 6 cups water and remaining ½ teaspoon salt to a boil in small saucepan over high heat. Stir in orzo. Reduce heat to medium-low; simmer 15 minutes or until tender. Drain orzo; stir in butter and parsley. Set aside and keep warm.

4 Thread beef onto skewers.

5 Grill skewers over medium-high heat 8 to 10 minutes, turning occasionally. Serve over orzo; garnish with fresh rosemary.

TIP

Rosemary skewers and brushes add the wonderful scent of rosemary to grilled foods. To make rosemary skewers, use large heavy sprigs and remove the leaves from the bottom three quarters of the sprigs. Thread small pieces of meat onto each sprig before grilling. Or, to make an aromatic brush, bundle sprigs of rosemary together and tie with kitchen string. Use as a brush for spreading sauces and glazes over meat or fish.

MEDITERRANEAN BURGERS
MAKES 4 SERVINGS

1½ pounds ground beef

 2 tablespoons grated Parmesan cheese

 2 tablespoons chopped kalamata olives

 1 tablespoon chopped fresh parsley

 1 tablespoon diced tomato

 2 teaspoons dried oregano

 1 teaspoon black pepper

 4 slices mozzarella cheese

 4 hamburger buns, split

   Roasted red pepper slices (optional)

1 Prepare grill for direct cooking.

2 Combine beef, Parmesan, olives, parsley, tomato, oregano and pepper in medium bowl; mix gently. Shape into four patties about ½ inch thick.

3 Grill patties, covered, over medium heat 4 to 5 minutes per side until cooked through (160°F) or to desired doneness. Top burgers with mozzarella just before placing on buns.

4 Serve burgers on buns with roasted peppers, if desired.

FLANK STEAK WITH ITALIAN SALSA
MAKES 6 SERVINGS

2 tablespoons olive oil

2 teaspoons balsamic vinegar

1 lean flank steak (1½ pounds)

1 tablespoon minced garlic

¾ teaspoon salt, divided

¾ teaspoon black pepper, divided

1 cup diced plum tomatoes

⅓ cup chopped pitted kalamata olives

2 tablespoons chopped fresh basil

1 Whisk oil and vinegar in medium bowl until well blended. Place steak in shallow dish; spread with garlic. Sprinkle with ½ teaspoon salt and ½ teaspoon pepper; drizzle with 2 tablespoons vinegar mixture. Marinate in refrigerator at least 20 minutes or up to 2 hours.

2 Prepare grill for direct cooking.

3 Add tomatoes, olives, basil, remaining ¼ teaspoon salt and ¼ teaspoon pepper to remaining vinegar mixture in medium bowl; mix well.

4 Drain steak; discard marinade. (Do not remove garlic from steak.)

5 Grill steak over medium-high heat 5 to 6 minutes per side for medium rare (145°F) or to desired doneness. Transfer steak to cutting board. Tent with foil; let stand 10 minutes. Cut across the grain into thin slices. Serve with salsa.

KOREAN BEEF SHORT RIBS
MAKES 4 TO 6 SERVINGS

2½ pounds beef chuck flanken-style short ribs, cut ⅜ to ½ inch thick*

¼ cup chopped green onions

¼ cup water

¼ cup soy sauce

1 tablespoon sugar

2 teaspoons grated fresh ginger

2 teaspoons dark sesame oil

2 cloves garlic, minced

½ teaspoon black pepper

1 tablespoon sesame seeds, toasted**

Flanken-style ribs can be ordered from your butcher. They are cross-cut short ribs sawed through the bones.

**To toast sesame seeds, place in small skillet. Shake skillet over medium-low heat about 3 minutes or until seeds begin to pop and turn golden.*

1 Place ribs in large resealable food storage bag. Combine green onions, water, soy sauce, sugar, ginger, oil, garlic and pepper in small bowl; pour over ribs. Seal bag; turn to coat. Marinate in refrigerator at least 4 hours or up to 8 hours, turning occasionally.

2 Prepare grill for direct cooking. Remove ribs from marinade; reserve marinade.

3 Grill ribs, covered, over medium-high heat 5 minutes. Brush lightly with reserved marinade; turn and brush again. Discard remaining marinade. Grill, covered, 5 to 6 minutes for medium or to desired doneness. Sprinkle with sesame seeds.

BEEF AND BEER SLIDERS
MAKES 12 SLIDERS

6 tablespoons ketchup
2 tablespoons mayonnaise
2 teaspoons Dijon mustard
1½ pounds ground beef
½ cup beer
1 teaspoon salt
½ teaspoon garlic powder
½ teaspoon onion powder
½ teaspoon dried oregano
½ teaspoon ground cumin
¼ teaspoon black pepper
3 slices sharp Cheddar cheese, cut into 4 pieces
12 slider buns or potato dinner rolls
12 baby lettuce leaves
12 plum tomato slices

1 Combine ketchup, mayonnaise and mustard in small bowl; mix well. Set aside.

2 Combine beef, beer, salt, garlic powder, onion powder, oregano, cumin and pepper in medium bowl; mix gently. Shape into 12 patties about ¼ inch thick.

3 Prepare grill for direct cooking. Oil grid.

4 Grill half of patties over medium-high heat 2 minutes. Turn and top each patty with one piece of cheese. Grill 2 minutes or until cheese is melted and patties are cooked through (160°F). Remove to large plate; keep warm. Repeat with remaining patties and cheese.

5 Serve bugers on buns with lettuce, tomato and ketchup mixture.

CHIPOTLE STRIP STEAKS
MAKES 4 SERVINGS

1 tablespoon olive oil

⅓ cup finely chopped onion

¾ cup beer

1 teaspoon Worcestershire sauce

⅓ cup ketchup

1 tablespoon red wine vinegar

1 teaspoon sugar

⅛ to ¼ teaspoon chipotle chile powder

4 bone-in strip steaks (8 to 9 ounces each)

1 teaspoon salt

1 Heat oil in small saucepan over medium-high heat. Add onion; cook 3 minutes or until softened, stirring occasionally. Add beer and Worcestershire sauce; bring to a boil, stirring occasionally. Cook until reduced to about ⅓ cup. Stir in ketchup, vinegar, sugar and chipotle chile powder; simmer over medium-low heat 3 minutes or until thickened, stirring occasionally. Keep warm.

2 Prepare grill for direct cooking. Oil grid. Sprinkle steaks with salt.

3 Grill steaks over medium-high heat 4 to 5 minutes per side for medium rare (145°F) or to desired doneness. Serve with chipotle sauce.

PEPPERED BEEF RIB-EYE ROAST
MAKES 6 TO 8 SERVINGS

1½ tablespoons black peppercorns

1 boneless beef rib-eye roast (2½ to 3 pounds), well trimmed

¼ cup Dijon mustard

2 cloves garlic, minced

Sour Cream Sauce (recipe follows)

1 Prepare grill for indirect cooking with drip pan in center of grill.

2 Place peppercorns in small resealable food storage bag. Squeeze out excess air; seal bag. Pound peppercorns using flat side of meat mallet or rolling pin until cracked.

3 Pat roast dry with paper towels. Combine mustard and garlic in small bowl; spread over roast. Sprinkle with cracked pepper.

4 Place roast on grid directly over drip pan. Grill, covered, over medium heat 1 hour or until medium rare (135°F), medium (150°F) or to desired doneness. Transfer to cutting board. Tent with foil; let stand 10 to 15 minutes before slicing. (Internal temperature will continue to rise 5°F to 10°F during stand time.)

5 Meanwhile, prepare Sour Cream Sauce. Slice roast; serve with sauce.

SOUR CREAM SAUCE
MAKES ABOUT 1 CUP

¾ cup sour cream

2 tablespoons prepared horseradish

1 tablespoon balsamic vinegar

½ teaspoon sugar

Combine all ingredients in small bowl; mix well.

BEER-MARINATED STEAK
MAKES 3 TO 4 SERVINGS

1½ pounds boneless beef top sirloin steak, ¾ inch thick
1 cup beer*
1 onion, finely chopped
½ cup soy sauce
¼ teaspoon black pepper
¼ cup (1 ounce) shredded Cheddar cheese (optional)

Do not use reduced-calorie light beer.

1 Place steak in large resealable food storage bag. Combine beer, onion, soy sauce and pepper in medium bowl; pour over steak. Seal bag; turn to coat. Marinate in refrigerator at least 8 hours or overnight, turning occasionally.

2 Prepare grill for direct cooking. Remove steak from marinade; discard marinade.

3 Grill steak, covered, over medium-high heat 4 to 5 minutes per side for medium rare (145°F) or to desired doneness. If desired, sprinkle steak with cheese just before removing from grill. Transfer to cutting board. Tent with foil; let stand 5 minutes before slicing.

4 Cut steak across the grain into thin slices.

SERVING SUGGESTION

Serve with sautéed vegetables and cilantro-lime rice. For vegetables, thinly slice 1 red onion, 1 red bell pepper and 1 green bell pepper. Heat 1 tablespoon oil in a large nonstick skillet over high heat. Add vegetables; cook and stir about 5 minutes or until vegetables are softened and browned. For rice, stir ¼ cup chopped fresh cilantro and 2 tablespoons lime juice into 3 cups hot cooked rice. Season with salt.

BACKYARD BARBECUE BURGERS
MAKES 6 SERVINGS

1½ pounds ground beef
⅓ cup barbecue sauce, divided
1 onion, cut into thick slices
1 tomato, sliced
2 tablespoons olive oil
6 Kaiser rolls, split
6 leaves green or red leaf lettuce

1 Prepare grill for direct cooking.

2 Combine beef and 2 tablespoons barbecue sauce in large bowl. Shape into six (1-inch-thick) patties.

3 Grill patties, covered, over medium heat 4 to 5 minutes per side until cooked through (160°F) or to desired doneness. Brush both sides with remaining barbecue sauce during last 5 minutes of cooking.

4 Meanwhile, brush onion and tomato slices with oil. Grill onion slices about 10 minutes and tomato slices 2 to 3 minutes, turning once.

5 Just before serving, grill rolls, cut sides down, until lightly toasted. Serve burgers on rolls with tomato, onion and lettuce.

PEPPERCORN STEAKS
MAKES 4 SERVINGS

2 tablespoons olive oil

1 to 2 teaspoons cracked pink or black peppercorns or ground black pepper

1 teaspoon dried herbs, such as rosemary or parsley

1 teaspoon minced garlic

4 boneless beef top loin (strip) or rib-eye steaks (6 ounces each)

¼ teaspoon salt

1 Combine oil, peppercorns, herbs and garlic in small bowl; mix well. Rub mixture on both sides of steaks. Place on plate; cover and refrigerate 30 to 60 minutes.

2 Prepare grill for direct cooking.

3 Grill steaks over medium heat 5 to 6 minutes per side until medium rare (145°F), medium (160°F) or to desired doneness. Season with salt.

PORK & LAMB

PORK FAJITAS WITH MANGO AND SALSA VERDE

MAKES 4 SERVINGS

2 cloves garlic, crushed

2 teaspoons chili powder

½ teaspoon ground cumin

½ teaspoon ground coriander

12 ounces pork tenderloin

1 medium red onion, cut into ½-inch rings

1 mango, peeled and cut into ½-inch pieces

8 (6-inch) flour tortillas, warmed

½ cup salsa verde (green salsa)

1 Prepare grill for direct cooking. Oil grid.

2 Combine garlic, chili powder, cumin and coriander in small bowl; mix well. Rub mixture all over pork.

3 Grill pork over medium-high heat 12 to 16 minutes or until 145°F, turning occasionally. During last 8 minutes of grilling, grill onion until tender, turning occasionally. Transfer pork to cutting board. Tent with foil; let stand 10 minutes before slicing.

4 Cut pork into ½-inch strips. Divide pork, onion and mango among tortillas; top with salsa verde. Fold bottom 3 inches of each tortilla up over filling; roll up to enclose filling.

GRILLED PORK CHOPS WITH LAGER BARBECUE SAUCE

MAKES 4 SERVINGS

4 bone-in, center-cut pork chops, 1 inch thick (2 to 2¼ pounds)

1 cup lager

⅓ cup maple syrup

3 tablespoons molasses

1 teaspoon Mexican-style hot chili powder

Lager Barbecue Sauce (recipe follows)

¾ teaspoon salt

¼ teaspoon black pepper

1 Place pork chops in large resealable food storage bag. Combine lager, maple syrup, molasses and chili powder in medium bowl; pour over pork. Seal bag; turn to coat. Marinate in refrigerator 2 hours, turning occasionally.

2 Prepare grill for direct cooking. Oil grid. Prepare Lager Barbecue Sauce.

3 Remove pork from marinade; discard marinade. Sprinkle with salt and pepper.

4 Grill pork over medium-high heat 6 to 7 minutes per side or until 145°F. Serve with sauce.

LAGER BARBECUE SAUCE

MAKES ABOUT ½ CUP

½ cup lager

⅓ cup ketchup

3 tablespoons maple syrup

2 tablespoons finely chopped onion

1 tablespoon molasses

1 tablespoon cider vinegar

½ teaspoon Mexican-style hot chili powder

Combine all ingredients in small saucepan; bring to a gentle simmer over medium heat. Cook 10 to 12 minutes or until slightly thickened, stirring occationally.

MINT MARINATED RACKS OF LAMB
MAKES 4 SERVINGS

2 whole racks (6 ribs each) lamb rib chops, well trimmed (about 3 pounds)

1 cup dry red wine

½ cup plus 2 tablespoons chopped fresh mint, divided

3 cloves garlic, minced

¼ cup Dijon mustard

⅔ cup plain dry bread crumbs

1 Place lamb in large resealable food storage bag. Combine wine, ½ cup mint and garlic in medium bowl; pour over lamb. Seal bag; turn to coat. Marinate in refrigerator at least 2 hours or up to 4 hours, turning occasionally.

2 Prepare grill for indirect cooking.

3 Remove lamb from marinade; discard marinade. Pat lamb dry with paper towels; place in shallow dish or plate. Combine mustard and remaining 2 tablespoons mint in small bowl; spread over meaty side of lamb. Pat bread crumbs evenly over mustard mixture.

4 Place lamb, crumb side down, on grid. Grill, covered, over medium heat 10 minutes. Turn and grill, covered, 20 minutes for medium or to desired doneness. Remove to cutting board. Tent with foil; let stand 10 minutes.

5 Slice lamb between ribs into individual chops.

APRICOT AND HONEY GLAZED BABY BACK RIBS

MAKES 6 TO 8 SERVINGS

1 tablespoon garlic powder

1 tablespoon ground cumin

1 teaspoon salt

½ teaspoon black pepper

6 pounds pork baby back ribs (2 racks), halved

1 bottle (12 ounces) honey wheat lager

1 cup apricot preserves

3 tablespoons honey

1 Prepare grill for indirect cooking. Oil grid.

2 Combine garlic powder, cumin, salt and pepper in small bowl; mix well. Rub mixture over both sides of ribs.

3 Grill ribs, meaty side down, over medium heat 30 minutes. Turn and grill 30 minutes.

4 Meanwhile, combine lager, preserves and honey in medium saucepan; bring to a boil over medium-high heat. Cook 20 minutes or until sauce thickens and is reduced to ¾ cup, stirring occasionally.

5 Turn and brush ribs with half of glaze; grill 15 minutes. Turn and brush with remaining glaze; grill 15 minutes or until ribs are tender.

PORK TENDERLOIN WITH APPLE SALSA
MAKES 4 SERVINGS

1 tablespoon chili powder

½ teaspoon garlic powder

1 pound pork tenderloin

2 Granny Smith apples, peeled and finely chopped

1 can (4 ounces) diced green chiles

¼ cup lemon juice

3 tablespoons finely chopped fresh cilantro

1 clove garlic, minced

1 teaspoon dried oregano

½ teaspoon salt

Fresh cilantro sprigs (optional)

1 Prepare grill for direct cooking. Oil grid.

2 Combine chili powder and garlic powder in small bowl; mix well. Rub mixture all over pork.

3 Grill pork over medium-high heat 30 minutes or until 145°F, turning occasionally. Transfer to cutting board. Tent with foil; let stand 10 to 15 minutes before slicing.

4 Meanwhile, combine apples, chiles, lemon juice, chopped cilantro, garlic, oregano and salt in medium bowl; mix well.

5 Slice pork; serve with salsa. Garnish with cilantro sprigs.

BEER-BRINED PORK CHOPS
MAKES 4 SERVINGS

1 bottle (12 ounces) dark beer

¼ cup packed dark brown sugar

1 tablespoon salt

1 tablespoon chili powder

2 cloves garlic, minced

3 cups ice water

4 pork chops (1 inch thick)

Grilled Rosemary Potatoes (optional)

1 Combine beer, brown sugar, salt, chili powder and garlic in medium bowl; stir until salt dissolves. Add ice water; stir until ice melts. Add pork chops; place medium plate on top to keep pork submerged in brine. Refrigerate 3 to 4 hours.

2 Prepare grill for direct cooking. Remove pork from brine; discard brine. Pat pork dry with paper towels. Prepare Grilled Rosemary Potatoes, if desired.

3 Grill pork, covered, over medium heat 10 to 12 minutes or until barely pink in center.

TIP

Brining adds flavor and moisture to meats. Be sure that your pork chops have not been injected with a sodium solution (check the package label) or they will be too salty.

GRILLED ROSEMARY POTATOES

Combine 4 quartered potatoes, ¼ cup chopped onion, 2 teaspoons chopped fresh rosemary and 1 teaspoon red pepper flakes on a 13×9-inch piece of heavy-duty foil; toss to coat. Top with an additional 13×9-inch piece of foil; seal edges of foil to make a packet. Grill 12 to 15 minutes or until potatoes are tender. Makes 4 servings.

PORK TENDERLOIN SLIDERS
MAKES 12 SANDWICHES

2 teaspoons chili powder

¾ teaspoon ground cumin

½ teaspoon salt

½ teaspoon black pepper

2 pork tenderloins (about 1 pound each)

2 tablespoons olive oil, divided

12 green onions, ends trimmed

½ cup mayonnaise

1 canned chipotle pepper in adobo sauce, minced

2 teaspoons lime juice

12 dinner rolls, sliced in half horizontally

12 slices Monterey Jack cheese

1 Prepare grill for direct cooking.

2 Combine chili powder, cumin, salt and black pepper in small bowl; mix well. Rub pork with 1 tablespoon oil; sprinkle with cumin mixture. Brush remaining 1 tablespoon oil over green onions.

3 Combine mayonnaise, chipotle and lime juice is small bowl; mix well. Cover and refrigerate until ready to use.

4 Grill pork, covered, over medium heat 15 minutes or until 145°F, turning occasionally. Transfer to cutting board. Tent with foil; let stand 10 minutes.

5 Meanwhile, grill green onions 3 minutes or until browned, turning frequently.

6 Coarsely chop green onions. Thinly slice pork. Spread mayonnaise mixture on bottom halves of rolls; top with green onions, pork and cheese. Serve immediately.

GREEK LAMB BURGERS
MAKES 4 SERVINGS

¼ cup pine nuts

¼ cup plain yogurt

3 cloves garlic, minced, divided

¼ teaspoon sugar

1 pound ground lamb

¼ cup finely chopped yellow onion

¾ teaspoon salt

¼ teaspoon black pepper

4 slices red onion (¼ inch thick)

1 tablespoon olive oil

8 slices pumpernickel bread

4 slices tomato

12 thin slices cucumber

1 Cook pine nuts in small skillet over medium heat 1 to 2 minutes or until lightly browned, stirring frequently. Remove to large bowl.

2 Prepare grill for direct cooking. Oil grid.

3 Combine yogurt, 1 clove garlic and sugar in small bowl; mix well. Add lamb, yellow onion, remaining 2 cloves garlic, salt and pepper to bowl with pine nuts; mix gently. Shape into four patties about 4 inches in diameter and ½ inch thick. Brush one side of each patty and red onion slice with oil.

4 Place patties and onion slices on grid, oil side down. Brush tops with oil. Grill, covered, over medium-high heat 4 to 5 minutes per side until patties are cooked through (160°F) or to desired doneness. Grill bread 1 to 2 minutes per side during last few minutes of grilling.

5 Serve burgers on bread with red onion, tomato, cucumber and yogurt sauce.

ASIAN-INSPIRED PORK AND NECTARINE KABOBS
MAKES 4 SERVINGS

1 pork tenderloin (about 1 pound)
¾ cup pineapple juice
3 tablespoons reduced-sodium soy sauce
1 tablespoon grated fresh ginger
1 teaspoon minced garlic
1 teaspoon ground cumin
1 teaspoon chili powder
½ teaspoon black pepper
3 fresh medium nectarines

1 Cut pork tenderloin in half lengthwise. Cut each half into eight pieces (16 pieces total). Place pork in large resealable food storage bag.

2 Combine pineapple juice, soy sauce, ginger, garlic, cumin, chili powder and pepper in medium bowl; pour over pork. Seal bag; turn to coat. Marinate in refrigerator 3 to 6 hours.

3 Soak eight wooden skewer in water 20 minutes. Prepare grill for direct cooking. Cut each nectarine into eight pieces. Remove pork from marinade; discard marinade. Thread pork and nectarines onto skewers.

4 Grill skewers over medium heat 9 to 12 minutes or until pork is barely pink in center, turning once.

SEASONED BABY BACK RIBS
MAKES 6 SERVINGS

 1 tablespoon paprika
1½ teaspoons garlic salt
 1 teaspoon celery salt
 ½ teaspoon black pepper
 ¼ teaspoon ground red pepper
 4 pounds pork baby back ribs, cut into 3- to 4-rib portions, well trimmed
   Barbecue Sauce (recipe follows)

1 Preheat oven to 350°F. Line shallow roasting pan with foil. Combine paprika, garlic salt, celery salt, black pepper and red pepper in small bowl; mix well. Rub mixture over both sides of ribs. Place ribs in prepared pan.

2 Bake 30 minutes. Meanwhile, prepare grill for direct cooking. Prepare Barbecue Sauce.

3 Grill ribs, covered, over medium heat 10 minutes. Brush half of Barbecue Sauce over both sides of ribs. Grill, covered, 10 minutes or until ribs are tender and browned. Serve with reserved sauce.

BARBECUE SAUCE
MAKES ABOUT ⅔ CUP

 ½ cup ketchup
 ⅓ cup packed light brown sugar
 1 tablespoon cider vinegar
 2 teaspoons Worcestershire sauce
 2 teaspoons soy sauce

Combine all ingredients in small bowl; mix well.

HONEY-MUSTARD PULLED PORK SANDWICHES
MAKES 8 SERVINGS

1 tablespoon chili powder

2 teaspoons ground cumin

½ teaspoon salt

2 tablespoons yellow mustard

2 pounds bone-in pork shoulder roast

2 bottles (12 ounces each) beer, divided

¾ cup ketchup

3 tablespoons honey

2 tablespoons cider vinegar

8 soft sandwich rolls

24 bread and butter pickle chips

1 Prepare grill for indirect cooking.

2 Combine chili powder, cumin and salt in small bowl; mix well. Spread mustard all over pork; sprinkle with cumin mixture. Place pork on rack in disposable foil pan. Reserve ¾ cup beer; pour enough remaining beer into pan to just cover rack beneath pork.

3 Place foil pan on grid opposite heat source. Grill pork, covered, over medium-low heat 4 to 6 hours or until fork-tender. Transfer to cutting board. Tent with foil; let stand 15 minutes.

4 Combine reserved ¾ cup beer, ketchup, honey and vinegar in small saucepan; bring to a boil over medium-high heat. Reduce heat to medium; cook and stir until thickened.

5 Shred pork with two forks, discarding any bone, fat or connective tissue. Combine pork and sauce in medium bowl; toss gently to coat. Serve pork on rolls with pickles.

BALSAMIC GRILLED PORK CHOPS
MAKES 2 SERVINGS

2 tablespoons balsamic vinegar

2 tablespoons reduced-sodium soy sauce

2 teaspoons sugar

1 teaspoon Dijon mustard

⅛ teaspoon red pepper flakes

2 boneless pork chops, trimmed (about 12 ounces total)

1 Combine vinegar, soy sauce, sugar, mustard and red pepper flakes in small bowl; mix well. Reserve 1 tablespoon marinade for serving.

2 Place pork in large resealable food storage bag; pour remaining marinade over pork. Seal bag; turn to coat. Marinate in refrigerator 2 hours or up to 24 hours.

3 Prepare grill for direct cooking. Oil grid. Remove pork from marinade; discard marinade.

4 Grill pork over medium-high heat 5 to 6 minutes per side or until barely pink in center. Top with reserved marinade.

CUBANO BURGERS
MAKES 4 SERVINGS

1½ pounds ground pork

¼ cup minced green onions

3 tablespoons yellow mustard, divided

1 tablespoon minced garlic

2 teaspoons paprika

½ teaspoon black pepper

¼ teaspoon salt

8 slices Swiss cheese

4 bolillos or Kaiser rolls, split and toasted

8 slices sandwich-style dill pickles

¼ pound thinly sliced ham

1 Prepare grill for direct cooking.

2 Combine pork, green onions, 1 tablespoon mustard, garlic, paprika, pepper and salt in large bowl; mix gently. Shape into four patties about ¾ inch thick, shaping to fit rolls.

3 Grill patties, covered, over medium heat 4 to 5 minutes per side or until cooked through (160°F). Top each burger with 2 slices cheese during last 2 minutes of grilling.

4 Spread remaining 2 tablespoons mustard over cut sides of rolls. Top with pickles, burgers and ham.

• • • • • • • • • • • • • • • • • • • •

NOTE

A bolillo is an oval-shaped roll about 6 inches long with a crunchy crust and a soft inside. If you can't find bolillos, use a loaf of French bread, cut in half lenthwise and then into individual-sized portions.

MARINATED ITALIAN SAUSAGE AND PEPPERS
MAKES 4 SERVINGS

4 links hot or sweet Italian sausage

1 large onion, cut into rings

1 large bell pepper, cut into quarters

½ cup olive oil

¼ cup red wine vinegar

2 tablespoons chopped fresh parsley

1 tablespoon dried oregano

2 cloves garlic, crushed

1 teaspoon salt

1 teaspoon black pepper

Horseradish-Mustard Spread (recipe follows)

1 Place sausage, onion and bell pepper in large resealable food storage bag. Combine oil, vinegar, parsley, oregano, garlic, salt and black pepper in small bowl; pour over sausage and vegetables. Seal bag; turn to coat. Marinate in refrigerator 1 to 2 hours.

2 Prepare grill for direct cooking. Prepare Horseradish-Mustard Spread; set aside. Remove sausage and vegetables from marinade; reserve marinade.

3 Grill sausage, covered, over medium heat 5 minutes. Turn sausage and place onion and bell pepper on grid; brush with reserved marinade. Discard remaining marinade. Grill, covered, 5 minutes or until sausage is cooked through and vegetables are crisp-tender.

4 Serve sausage and vegetables with Horseradish-Mustard Spread.

HORSERADISH-MUSTARD SPREAD

Combine 3 tablespoons mayonnaise, 1 tablespoon chopped fresh parsley, 1 tablespoon prepared horseradish, 1 tablespoon Dijon mustard, 2 teaspoons garlic powder and 1 teaspoon black pepper in small bowl; mix well.

THAI-STYLE PORK KABOBS
MAKES 4 SERVINGS

⅓ cup reduced-sodium soy sauce

2 tablespoons fresh lime juice

2 tablespoons water

2 teaspoons hot chili oil*

2 cloves garlic, minced

1 teaspoon minced fresh ginger

12 ounces pork tenderloin, cut into ½-inch strips

1 small red bell pepper, cut into ½-inch pieces

1 small yellow bell pepper, cut into ½-inch pieces

1 red or sweet onion, cut into ½-inch pieces

2 cups hot cooked rice

If hot chili oil is not available, combine 2 teaspoons vegetable oil and ½ teaspoon red pepper flakes in small microwavable bowl. Microwave on HIGH 30 to 45 seconds; let stand 5 minutes to allow flavors to blend.

1 Combine soy sauce, lime juice, water, chili oil, garlic and ginger in medium bowl; mix well. Reserve ⅓ cup for dipping sauce. Add pork to remaining mixture; toss to coat. Cover and marinate in refrigerator at least 30 minutes or up to 2 hours, turning once.

2 Soak eight 8- to 10-inch wooden skewers in water 20 minutes. Prepare grill for direct cooking. Oil grid.

3 Remove pork from marinade; discard marinade. Alternately thread pork, bell peppers and onion onto skewers.

4 Grill skewers, covered, over medium heat 6 to 8 minutes or until pork is barely pink in center, turning once.

5 Serve with rice and reserved dipping sauce.

HERBED LAMB CHOPS
MAKES 4 TO 6 SERVINGS

8 lamb loin chops, 1 inch thick (about 2 pounds)

⅓ cup vegetable oil

⅓ cup red wine vinegar

2 tablespoons soy sauce

1 tablespoon lemon juice

3 cloves garlic, crushed

1 teaspoon salt

1 teaspoon chopped fresh oregano *or* ¼ teaspoon dried oregano

1 teaspoon dried rosemary

1 teaspoon ground mustard

½ teaspoon white pepper

1 Place lamb chops in large resealable food storage bag. Combine oil, vinegar, soy sauce, lemon juice, garlic, salt, oregano, rosemary, mustard and pepper in medium bowl; mix well. Reserve ½ cup marinade in small bowl; pour remaining marinade over lamb. Seal bag; turn to coat. Marinate in refrigerator at least 1 hour.

2 Prepare grill for direct cooking. Remove lamb from marinade; discard marinade.

3 Grill lamb over medium-high heat 8 minutes or to desired doneness, turning once and basting often with reserved ½ cup marinade. Do not baste during last 5 minutes of cooking. Discard any remaining marinade.

BODACIOUS GRILLED RIBS
MAKES 4 SERVINGS

4 pounds pork loin back ribs

2 tablespoons paprika

2 teaspoons dried basil

½ teaspoon onion powder

¼ teaspoon garlic powder

¼ teaspoon ground red pepper

¼ teaspoon black pepper

2 sheets (24×18 inches each) heavy-duty foil, lightly sprayed with nonstick cooking spray

8 ice cubes

1 cup barbecue sauce

½ cup apricot fruit spread

1 Prepare grill for direct cooking. Cut ribs into 4- to 6-rib portions.

2 Combine paprika, basil, onion powder, garlic powder, red pepper and black pepper in small bowl; mix well. Rub mixture over both sides of ribs. Place half of ribs in single layer in center of each foil sheet. Place 4 ice cubes on top of each layer of ribs.

3 Double-fold sides and ends of foil to seal packets, leaving head space for heat circulation.

4 Grill packets, covered, over medium heat 45 to 60 minutes or until ribs are tender. Carefully open one end of each packet to allow steam to escape.

5 Combine barbecue sauce and fruit spread in small bowl; mix well. Transfer ribs to grid; brush with barbecue sauce mixture. Grill 5 to 10 minutes, brushing with sauce and turning frequently.

POULTRY

SMOKED TURKEY BREAST WITH CHIPOTLE RUB
MAKES 8 TO 10 SERVINGS

  Mesquite or hickory wood chips

2 tablespoons packed dark brown sugar

2 tablespoons ground cumin

1 tablespoon salt

1 tablespoon garlic powder

1 tablespoon smoked paprika

2 teaspoons ground red pepper

1 teaspoon chili powder

¼ cup butter, softened

1 bone-in skin-on turkey breast (5½ to 6 pounds)

1 Soak wood chips in water at least 30 minutes. Prepare grill for indirect cooking.

2 Combine brown sugar, cumin, salt, garlic powder, paprika, red pepper and chili powder in small bowl; mix well. Place 2 tablespoons spice mixture in another small bowl. Add butter; mix well.

3 Gently loosen skin of turkey breast. Spread butter mixture under skin onto breast. Rub skin and cavity of turkey with remaining spice mixture.

4 Remove some wood chips from water; place in small aluminum tray. Place tray under grill rack directly on heat source; allow wood to begin to smolder, about 10 minutes.

5 Grill turkey, covered, over medium-high heat 1 hour. Replenish wood chips after 1 hour. Grill until cooked through (165°F). Transfer to cutting board. Tent with foil; let stand 10 minutes before slicing.

GRILLED CHICKEN TOSTADAS
MAKES 4 SERVINGS

1 pound boneless skinless chicken breasts

1 teaspoon ground cumin

¼ cup plus 2 tablespoons salsa, divided

¼ cup fresh orange juice

2 tablespoons vegetable oil, divided

2 cloves garlic, minced

8 green onions

1 can (about 15 ounces) refried beans

4 (10-inch) or 8 (6- to 7-inch) flour tortillas

2 cups sliced romaine lettuce leaves

1½ cups (6 ounces) shredded pepper Jack cheese

1 ripe medium avocado, diced

1 medium tomato, seeded and coarsely chopped

Fresh cilantro sprigs (optional)

Sour cream

1 Place chicken in single layer in shallow glass dish; sprinkle with cumin. Combine ¼ cup salsa, orange juice, 1 tablespoon oil and garlic in small bowl; pour over chicken. Cover and marinate in refrigerator at least 2 hours or up to 8 hours, stirring occasionally.

2 Prepare grill for direct cooking. Remove chicken from marinade; reserve marinade. Brush green onions with remaining 1 tablespoon oil.

3 Grill chicken and green onions, covered, over medium heat 5 minutes. Brush chicken with half of reserved marinade; turn and brush with remaining marinade. Turn green onions. Grill, covered, 5 minutes or until chicken is no longer pink in center and green onions are tender. Transfer to cutting board. Let chicken stand 5 minutes before slicing.

4 Meanwhile, combine beans and remaining 2 tablespoons salsa in small saucepan; cook over medium heat until heated through, stirring occasionally.

5 Place tortillas in single layer on grid. Grill, uncovered, 1 to 2 minutes per side or until golden brown. (If tortillas puff up, pierce with tip of knife or flatten with spatula.)

6 Cut chicken crosswise into ½-inch strips. Cut green onions crosswise into 1-inch pieces. Spread tortillas with bean mixture; top with lettuce, chicken, green onions, cheese, avocado and tomato. Garnish with cilantro. Serve with sour cream.

GRILLED CHICKEN WITH CHIMICHURRI SALSA
MAKES 4 SERVINGS

4 boneless skinless chicken breasts (6 ounces each)

½ cup plus 4 teaspoons olive oil, divided

   Salt and black pepper

½ cup finely chopped fresh parsley

¼ cup white wine vinegar

2 tablespoons finely chopped onion

3 cloves garlic, minced

1 fresh or canned jalapeño pepper,* finely chopped

2 teaspoons dried oregano

Jalapeño peppers can sting and irritate the skin, so wear rubber gloves when handling peppers and do not touch your eyes.

1 Prepare grill for direct cooking. Brush chicken with 4 teaspoons oil; season with salt and black pepper.

2 Grill chicken, covered, over medium heat 5 to 7 minutes per side or until no longer pink in center.

3 Meanwhile, combine parsley, remaining ½ cup oil, vinegar, onion, garlic, jalapeño and oregano in medium bowl; mix well. Season with salt and black pepper. Serve over chicken.

TIP

Chimichurri salsa can be served with grilled steak or fish as well as chicken. Chimichurri will remain fresh tasting for up to 24 hours.

BBQ TURKEY MINIS
MAKES 12 MINI BURGERS

½ cup panko bread crumbs

½ cup barbecue sauce, divided

1 egg, beaten

1 pound ground turkey

1 package (12 ounces) Hawaiian bread rolls, split horizontally

Lettuce

Tomato slices

3 slices American cheese, quartered

1 Prepare grill for direct cooking. Oil grid.

2 Combine panko, ¼ cup barbecue sauce and egg in medium bowl; mix well. Add turkey; mix gently. Shape into 12 small patties about ½ inch thick (¼ cup per patty).

3 Grill patties, covered, over high heat 4 to 5 minutes per side or until cooked through (165°F). Brush with remaining ¼ cup barbecue sauce during last minute of cooking.

4 Serve burgers on rolls with lettuce, tomato and cheese.

TIP

The center of each burger should reach 160°F before being removed from the grill; the internal temperature will continue to rise to 165°F upon standing.

CHICKEN AND VEGETABLE SATAY WITH PEANUT SAUCE

MAKES 4 SERVINGS

1½ pounds boneless skinless chicken thighs, cut into 32 (1½-inch) cubes

⅔ cup Thai or other Asian beer, divided

3 tablespoons packed dark brown sugar, divided

1 tablespoon plus 2 teaspoons lime juice, divided

3 cloves garlic, minced and divided

1¼ teaspoons curry powder, divided

½ cup coconut milk

½ cup chunky peanut butter

1 tablespoon fish sauce

3 tablespoons peanut oil, divided

¼ cup finely chopped onion

24 medium mushrooms, stems trimmed

4 green onions, cut into 24 (1-inch) pieces

Hot cooked noodles or rice (optional)

1 Place chicken in large resealable food storage bag. Combine ⅓ cup beer, 1 tablespoon brown sugar, 1 tablespoon lime juice, 2 cloves garlic and 1 teaspoon curry powder in small bowl; pour over chicken. Seal bag; turn to coat. Marinate in refrigerator 2 hours, turning occasionally.

2 Meanwhile, combine remaining ⅓ cup beer, 2 tablespoons brown sugar, 2 teaspoons lime juice, coconut milk, peanut butter and fish sauce in medium bowl; mix well.

3 Heat 1 tablespoon oil in small saucepan over medium-high heat. Add onion and remaining 1 clove garlic; cook and stir 2 to 3 minutes or until onion begins to soften. Add remaining ¼ teaspoon curry powder; cook and stir 15 seconds. Stir in coconut milk mixture. Reduce heat to medium; simmer about 15 minutes or until thickened, stirring frequently. Keep warm.

4 Soak eight wooden skewers in water 20 minutes. Prepare grill for direct cooking. Oil grid.

5 Remove chicken from marinade; discard marinade. Alternately thread chicken, mushrooms and green onions onto eight skewers. Brush skewers with remaining 2 tablespoons oil.

6 Grill skewers over medium-high heat 8 to 10 minutes or until chicken is cooked through and mushrooms are tender, turning occasionally. Serve with peanut sauce. For a heartier meal, serve over noodles or rice, if desired.

GRILLED CHICKEN WITH CORN AND BLACK BEAN SALSA

MAKES 4 SERVINGS

½ cup corn

½ cup finely chopped red bell pepper

½ (15-ounce) can black beans, rinsed and drained

½ ripe medium avocado, diced

¼ cup chopped fresh cilantro

2 tablespoons lime juice

1 tablespoon chopped pickled jalapeño slices

½ teaspoon salt, divided

1 teaspoon black pepper

½ teaspoon chili powder

4 boneless skinless chicken breasts (4 ounces each), pounded to ½-inch thickness

1 Combine corn, bell pepper, beans, avocado, cilantro, lime juice, jalapeño and ¼ teaspoon salt in medium bowl; mix well.

2 Combine black pepper, remaining ¼ teaspoon salt and chili powder in small bowl; mix well. Sprinkle over both sides of chicken.

3 Prepare grill for direct cooking. Oil grid.

4 Grill chicken over medium-high heat 4 minutes per side or until no longer pink in center. Serve with salsa.

THAI BARBECUED CHICKEN
MAKES 4 SERVINGS

1 cup coarsely chopped fresh cilantro

2 jalapeño peppers,* stemmed and seeded

8 cloves garlic, coarsely chopped

2 tablespoons fish sauce

1 tablespoon packed brown sugar

1 teaspoon curry powder

 Grated peel of 1 lemon

3 pounds bone-in chicken pieces

Jalapeño peppers can sting and irritate the skin, so wear rubber gloves when handling peppers and do not touch your eyes.

1 Combine cilantro, jalapeños, garlic, fish sauce, brown sugar, curry powder and lemon peel in food processor or blender; process until coarse paste forms.

2 Work fingers between skin and meat on breast and thigh pieces. Rub about 1 teaspoon seasoning paste under skin on each piece. Rub remaining paste all over chicken pieces. Place chicken in large resealable food storage bag; seal bag. Marinate in refrigerator 3 to 4 hours or overnight.

3 Prepare grill for direct cooking.

4 Grill chicken, skin side down, covered, over medium heat about 10 minutes or until well browned. Turn and grill 20 to 30 minutes or until chicken is cooked through (165°F). Thighs and legs may require 5 to 10 minutes more cooking time than breasts. If chicken is browned on both sides but still needs additional cooking, move to edge of grill, away from direct heat, to finish cooking.

BUFFALO CHICKEN DRUMSTICKS
MAKES 4 SERVINGS

8 large chicken drumsticks (about 2 pounds)

3 tablespoons hot pepper sauce

1 tablespoon vegetable oil

1 clove garlic, minced

¼ cup mayonnaise

3 tablespoons sour cream

1 tablespoon white wine vinegar

¼ teaspoon sugar

⅓ cup crumbled blue cheese

2 cups hickory chips

1 Place chicken in large resealable food storage bag. Combine hot pepper sauce, oil and garlic in small bowl; pour over chicken. Seal bag; turn to coat. Marinate in refrigerator at least 1 hour or up to 24 hours for spicier flavor, turning occasionally.

2 Combine mayonnaise, sour cream, vinegar and sugar in another small bowl; mix well. Stir in blue cheese; cover and refrigerate until ready to serve.

3 Soak hickory chips in cold water 20 minutes. Prepare grill for direct cooking. Remove chicken from marinade; discard marinade. Drain hickory chips; sprinkle over coals.

4 Grill chicken, covered, over medium-high heat 25 to 30 minutes or until cooked through (165°F), turning occasionally. Serve with blue cheese dressing.

HONEY MUSTARD GLAZED CHICKEN
MAKES 4 SERVINGS

1 whole chicken (4 to 5 pounds)

1 tablespoon vegetable oil

¼ cup honey

2 tablespoons Dijon mustard

1 tablespoon reduced-sodium soy sauce

½ teaspoon ground ginger

⅛ teaspoon salt

⅛ teaspoon black pepper

1 Prepare grill for indirect cooking.

2 Pull chicken skin over neck; secure with metal skewer. Tuck wings under back; tie legs together with wet kitchen string. Lightly brush chicken with oil.

3 Combine honey, mustard, soy sauce, ginger, salt and pepper in small bowl; mix well.

4 Place chicken, breast side up, on grid directly over drip pan. Grill, covered, over medium-high heat 1 hour 30 minutes or until cooked through (165°F), brushing with glaze every 10 minutes during last 30 minutes of cooking. Transfer to cutting board. Tent with foil; let stand 15 minutes before carving.

CHICKEN AND FRUIT KABOBS
MAKES 12 SERVINGS

1¾ cups honey

¾ cup lemon juice

½ cup Dijon mustard

⅓ cup minced fresh ginger

4 pounds boneless skinless chicken breasts, cut into 1-inch pieces

6 plums, pitted and quartered

3 firm bananas, cut into chunks

4 cups pineapple chunks (about half of medium pineapple)

1 Soak wooden skewers in water 20 minutes. Prepare grill for direct cooking.

2 Combine honey, lemon juice, mustard and ginger in small bowl; mix well. Alternately thread chicken and fruit onto skewers; brush generously with honey mixture.

3 Grill skewers about 10 minutes or until chicken is cooked through, turning and brushing frequently with remaining honey mixture.

GINGER-LIME CHICKEN THIGHS
MAKES 2 TO 4 SERVINGS

6 boneless skinless chicken thighs

⅓ cup vegetable oil

3 tablespoons lime juice

3 tablespoons honey

2 teaspoons grated fresh ginger *or* 1 teaspoon ground ginger

¼ to ½ teaspoon red pepper flakes

1 Place chicken in large resealable food storage bag. Combine oil, lime juice, honey, ginger and red pepper flakes in small bowl; mix well. Pour ½ cup marinade over chicken; reserve remaining marinade. Seal bag; turn to coat. Marinate in refrigerator 30 to 60 minutes, turning occasionally.

2 Prepare grill for direct cooking. Remove chicken from marinade; discard marinade.

3 Grill chicken over medium-high heat 12 minutes or until cooked through, turning once. Brush with reserved ½ cup marinade during last 5 minutes of cooking.

GRILLED CUBAN PARTY SANDWICH
MAKES 6 SANDWICHES

　2 boneless skinless chicken breasts (about 4 ounces each)
¾ cup plus 1 to 2 tablespoons olive oil, divided
　6 tablespoons lime juice
　4 cloves garlic, minced
2¼ teaspoons salt
　¾ teaspoon black pepper
　1 medium yellow onion, cut into ½-inch-thick slices (leave rings intact)
　1 loaf ciabatta bread (1 pound), cut in half horizontally
　¼ cup chopped fresh cilantro
　6 ounces fresh mozzarella, sliced
　1 medium tomato, thinly sliced

1 Place chicken in large resealable food storage bag. Combine ¾ cup oil, lime juice, garlic, 2¼ teaspoons salt and ¾ teaspoon pepper in medium bowl; mix well. Pour ¼ cup marinade over chicken; refrigerate remaining marinade. Seal bag; turn to coat. Marinate in refrigerator up to 2 hours.

2 Soak two wooden skewers in water 20 minutes. Prepare grill for direct cooking. Oil grid. Thread onion slices onto skewers. Remove chicken from marinade; discard marinade.

3 Grill chicken over medium heat 5 to 7 minutes per side or until no longer pink in center. Brush onions with 1 tablespoon oil; place on grid next to chicken. Grill onions 4 to 6 minutes per side or until soft and browned.

4 Transfer chicken and onions to cutting board. Let chicken stand 10 minutes before slicing. Lightly season onions with additional salt and pepper, remove from skewers and separate rings. Toast cut sides of bread on grill.

5 Place bread on cutting board, cut sides up. Stir reserved marinade; brush on both halves of bread. Sprinkle cilantro on bottom half; top with mozzarella, tomato, chicken, onions and top half of bread. Press down firmly. Wrap sandwich in foil.

6 Place sandwich on grid; top with large skillet to flatten, if desired. Grill 4 to 6 minutes or until cheese melts. Cut into six pieces. Serve immediately.

POLLO DIAVOLO (DEVILED CHICKEN)
MAKES 4 TO 6 SERVINGS

8 skinless bone-in chicken thighs (2½ to 3 pounds)

¼ cup olive oil

3 tablespoons lemon juice

6 cloves garlic, minced

1 to 2 teaspoons red pepper flakes

3 tablespoons butter, softened

1 teaspoon dried or rubbed sage

1 teaspoon dried thyme

¾ teaspoon coarse salt

¼ teaspoon ground red pepper or black pepper

Lemon wedges

1 Place chicken in large resealable food storage bag. Combine oil, lemon juice, garlic and red pepper flakes in small bowl; pour over chicken. Seal bag; turn to coat. Marinate in refrigerator at least 1 hour or up to 8 hours, turning once.

2 Prepare grill for direct cooking. Remove chicken from marinade; reserve marinade.

3 Place chicken on grid; brush with reserved marinade. Grill, covered, over medium-high heat 8 minutes. Turn and brush with remaining marinade. Grill, covered, 8 to 10 minutes or until cooked through (165°F).

4 Meanwhile, combine butter, sage, thyme, salt and ground red pepper in small bowl; mix well. Transfer chicken to serving platter; spread herb butter over chicken. Serve with lemon wedges.

CHIPOTLE SPICE-RUBBED BEER CAN CHICKEN
MAKES 4 SERVINGS

2 tablespoons packed brown sugar

2 teaspoons smoked paprika

2 teaspoons ground cumin

1 teaspoon salt

1 teaspoon garlic powder

1 teaspoon chili powder

½ teaspoon ground chipotle pepper

1 whole chicken (3½ to 4 pounds), patted dry

1 can (12 ounces) beer

1 Prepare grill for indirect cooking. Oil grid.

2 Combine brown sugar, paprika, cumin, salt, garlic powder, chili powder and chipotle pepper in small bowl; mix well. Gently loosen skin of chicken over breast, legs and thighs. Rub spice mixture under and over skin and inside cavity. Discard one fourth of beer. Hold chicken upright with cavity pointing down; insert beer can into cavity.

3 Place chicken on grid, standing upright on can. Spread legs slightly for support. Grill, covered, over medium heat 1 hour 15 minutes or until chicken is cooked through (165°F).

4 Lift chicken off beer can using metal tongs. Transfer to cutting board (keep chicken standing upright). Tent with foil; let stand 15 minutes before carving.

SPICED TURKEY WITH FRUIT SALSA
MAKES 2 SERVINGS

1 turkey breast tenderloin (about 6 ounces)

2 teaspoons lime juice

1 teaspoon mesquite seasoning blend or ground cumin

½ cup frozen pitted sweet cherries, thawed and halved*

¼ cup chunky salsa

Drained canned sweet cherries can be substituted for frozen cherries.

1 Prepare grill for direct cooking. Brush turkey with lime juice; sprinkle with mesquite seasoning.

2 Grill turkey, covered, over medium heat 15 to 20 minutes or until cooked through (165°F). Transfer to cutting board. Tent with foil; let stand 10 minutes before slicing.

3 Meanwhile, combine cherries and salsa in small bowl; mix well. Thinly slice turkey; serve with salsa.

GRILLED CHICKEN ADOBO
MAKES 6 SERVINGS

½ cup chopped onion

⅓ cup lime juice

6 cloves garlic, coarsely chopped

1 teaspoon ground cumin

1 teaspoon dried oregano

½ teaspoon dried thyme

¼ teaspoon ground red pepper

6 boneless skinless chicken breasts (about ¼ pound each)

3 tablespoons chopped fresh cilantro (optional)

1 Combine onion, lime juice and garlic in food processor; process until onion is finely minced. Transfer to large resealable food storage bag. Add cumin, oregano, thyme and red pepper; knead bag until blended. Add chicken to bag. Seal bag; turn to coat. Marinate in refrigerator 30 minutes or up to 4 hours, turning occasionally.

2 Prepare grill for direct cooking. Oil grid. Remove chicken from marinade; discard marinade.

3 Grill chicken over medium heat 5 to 7 minutes per side or until no longer pink in center. Sprinkle with cilantro, if desired.

JAMAICAN RUM CHICKEN
MAKES 6 SERVINGS

6 boneless skinless chicken breasts

½ cup dark rum

2 tablespoons packed brown sugar

2 tablespoons lime juice or lemon juice

2 tablespoons soy sauce

4 cloves garlic, minced

1 to 2 jalapeño peppers,* seeded and minced

1 tablespoon minced fresh ginger

1 teaspoon dried thyme

½ teaspoon black pepper

Jalapeño peppers can sting and irritate the skin, so wear rubber gloves when handling peppers and do not touch your eyes.

1 Place chicken in large resealable food storage bag. Combine rum, brown sugar, lime juice, soy sauce, garlic, jalapeño, ginger, thyme and black pepper in small bowl; pour over chicken. Seal bag; turn to coat. Marinate in refrigerator 4 hours or overnight, turning once or twice.

2 Prepare grill for direct cooking. Remove chicken from marinade; reserve marinade.

3 Grill chicken, covered, over medium heat 5 to 7 minutes per side or until no longer pink in center.

4 Meanwhile, bring remaining marinade to a boil in small saucepan over medium-high heat. Boil 5 minutes or until marinade is reduced by about half. Drizzle marinade over chicken.

SEAFOOD

BEER AND ORANGE MARINATED TUNA STEAKS
MAKES 4 SERVINGS

NECTARINE SALSA

2 large nectarines, pitted and cut into ½-inch pieces

3 tablespoons finely chopped red onion

2 tablespoons chopped fresh cilantro

½ jalapeño pepper,* finely chopped

1 tablespoon lime juice

¼ teaspoon salt

TUNA

½ cup beer

⅓ cup finely chopped green onions

¼ cup orange juice

¼ cup reduced-sodium soy sauce

2 tablespoons lemon juice

2 tablespoons sugar

2 tablespoons grated fresh ginger

2 cloves garlic, minced

4 (6- to 8-ounce) tuna steaks, about ¾ inch thick

Jalapeño peppers can sting and irritate the skin, so wear rubber gloves when handling peppers and do not touch your eyes.

1 Combine nectarines, red onion, cilantro, jalapeño, lime juice and salt in medium bowl; mix well.

2 Combine beer, green onions, orange juice, soy sauce, lemon juice, sugar, ginger and garlic in large bowl; mix well. Add tuna; turn to coat. Marinate in refrigerator 30 minutes, turning occasionally.

3 Prepare grill for direct cooking. Oil grid. Remove tuna from marinade; discard marinade.

4 Grill tuna over medium-high heat 3 minutes per side or until pink in center. Serve with salsa.

SALMON, ASPARAGUS AND ORZO SALAD
MAKES 4 TO 6 SERVINGS

1 cup uncooked orzo pasta

1 salmon fillet (8 ounces)

8 ounces asparagus, cooked and cut into 2-inch pieces (about 1½ cups)

½ cup dried cranberries

¼ cup sliced green onions

3 tablespoons extra virgin olive oil

1 tablespoon white wine vinegar

1½ teaspoons Dijon mustard

½ teaspoon salt

⅛ teaspoon black pepper

1 Prepare grill for direct cooking. Oil grid.

2 Cook orzo according to package directions; drain and cool.

3 Grill salmon over medium heat about 10 minutes per inch of thickness or until center is opaque. Remove to plate; flake into bite-size pieces.

4 Combine salmon, orzo, asparagus, cranberries and green onions in large bowl. Combine oil, vinegar, mustard, salt and pepper in small bowl; mix well. Pour dressing over salmon mixture; toss gently to coat. Cover and refrigerate 30 minutes to 1 hour before serving.

LEMON ROSEMARY SHRIMP AND VEGETABLE SOUVLAKI
MAKES 4 SERVINGS

3 tablespoons extra virgin olive oil, divided

2 tablespoons lemon juice

2 teaspoons grated lemon peel

2 cloves garlic, minced

½ teaspoon salt

½ teaspoon finely chopped fresh rosemary

⅛ teaspoon red pepper flakes

8 ounces large raw shrimp, peeled and deveined (with tails on)

1 medium zucchini, halved lengthwise and cut into ½-inch slices

½ medium red bell pepper, cut into 1-inch pieces

8 green onions, trimmed and cut into 2-inch pieces

1 Soak four 12-inch wooden skewers in water 20 minutes. Prepare grill for direct cooking. Oil grid.

2 Combine 2 tablespoons oil, lemon juice, lemon peel, garlic, salt, rosemary and red pepper flakes in small bowl; mix well.

3 Alternately thread shrimp, zucchini, bell pepper and green onions onto skewers. Brush both sides of skewers with remaining 1 tablespoon oil.

4 Grill skewers over medium heat 4 to 6 minutes or until shrimp are pink and opaque, turning once. Remove to serving platter; drizzle with sauce.

NOTE

"Souvlaki" is the Greek word for shish kebab. Souvlaki traditionally consists of fish or meat that has been seasoned in a mixture of oil, lemon juice and seasonings. Many souvlaki recipes also include chunks of vegetables such as bell pepper and onion.

. . . .

TUNA, FENNEL AND PASTA SALAD
MAKES 4 SERVINGS

Balsamic Vinaigrette (recipe follows)

¾ pound tuna steaks

2 teaspoons Dijon mustard

8 ounces uncooked small shell pasta, cooked and drained

4 cups torn red leaf lettuce

2 cups sliced asparagus, cooked crisp-tender and cooled

½ cup thinly sliced fennel

½ cup thinly sliced red bell pepper

8 cherry tomatoes, halved

Salt and black pepper

1 Prepare grill for direct cooking. Prepare Balsamic Vinaigrette. Brush both sides of tuna with mustard.

2 Grill tuna over medium-high heat about 5 minutes per side or until fish begins to flake when tested with fork. Remove to plate; break into chunks.

3 Combine tuna, pasta, lettuce, asparagus, fennel, bell pepper and tomatoes in large bowl. Drizzle with Balsamic Vinaigrette; toss gently to coat. Season with salt and black pepper.

BALSAMIC VINAIGRETTE
MAKES ABOUT ⅔ CUP

¼ cup water

¼ cup balsamic vinegar

3 tablespoons olive oil

2 tablespoons finely chopped red or green onion

3 cloves garlic, minced

¾ teaspoon dried chervil

½ teaspoon salt

½ teaspoon celery seeds

Combine all ingredients in small jar with tight-fitting lid; refrigerate until ready to use. Shake well before using.

HOT SHRIMP WITH COOL MELON SALSA
MAKES 4 SERVINGS

¼ cup prepared salsa

4 tablespoons lime juice, divided

1 teaspoon honey

1 clove garlic, minced

2 to 4 drops hot pepper sauce

1 pound large raw shrimp, peeled and deveined (with tails on)

1 cup finely diced honeydew melon

½ cup finely diced unpeeled cucumber

2 tablespoons minced fresh parsley

1 green onion, finely chopped

1½ teaspoons sugar

1 teaspoon olive oil

¼ teaspoon salt

1 Soak wooden skewers in water 20 minutes. Prepare grill for direct cooking.

2 Combine salsa, 2 tablespoons lime juice, honey, garlic and hot pepper sauce in small bowl; mix well. Thread shrimp onto skewers; brush with salsa mixture.

3 Combine remaining 2 tablespoons lime juice, honeydew, cucumber, parsley, green onion, sugar, oil and salt in medium bowl; mix well.

4 Grill skewers over medium heat 4 to 6 minutes or until shrimp are pink and opaque, turning once. Serve with salsa.

SZECHUAN TUNA STEAKS
MAKES 4 SERVINGS

4 tuna steaks (6 ounces each), cut 1 inch thick

¼ cup dry sherry or sake

¼ cup soy sauce

1 tablespoon dark sesame oil

1 teaspoon hot chili oil *or* ¼ teaspoon red pepper flakes

1 clove garlic, minced

3 tablespoons chopped fresh cilantro (optional)

1 Place tuna in single layer in large shallow glass dish. Combine sherry, soy sauce, sesame oil, hot chili oil and garlic in small bowl; mix well. Reserve ¼ cup marinade at room temperature. Pour remaining marinade over tuna; cover and marinate in refrigerator 40 minutes, turning once.

2 Prepare grill for direct cooking. Oil grid. Remove tuna from marinade; discard marinade.

3 Grill tuna over medium-high heat 3 minutes per side or until tuna is seared but still feels somewhat soft in center.* Transfer to cutting board; let stand 5 minutes.

4 Cut tuna steaks into thin slices; fan out slices onto serving plates. Drizzle with reserved marinade; sprinkle with cilantro, if desired.

Tuna becomes dry and tough if overcooked. Cook to medium doneness for best results.

GRILLED RED SNAPPER WITH AVOCADO-PAPAYA SALSA

MAKES 4 SERVINGS

1 teaspoon ground coriander

1 teaspoon paprika

¾ teaspoon salt

⅛ to ¼ teaspoon ground red pepper

½ cup diced ripe avocado

½ cup diced ripe papaya

2 tablespoons chopped fresh cilantro

1 tablespoon lime juice

1 tablespoon olive oil

4 skinless red snapper or halibut fillets (5 to 7 ounces each)

4 lime wedges

1 Prepare grill for direct cooking. Oil grid.

2 Combine coriander, paprika, salt and red pepper in small bowl; mix well. Combine avocado, papaya, cilantro, lime juice and ¼ teaspoon spice mixture in medium bowl; set aside.

3 Brush oil over snapper; sprinkle both sides with remaining spice mixture.

4 Grill snapper, covered, over medium-high heat 10 minutes or until fish begins to flake when tested with fork, turning once. Serve with salsa and lime wedges.

BARBECUED SHRIMP OVER TROPICAL RICE
MAKES 4 SERVINGS

½ cup uncooked brown rice

20 frozen large raw shrimp (26 to 30 per pound), thawed according to package directions, peeled and deveined (with tails on)

½ cup barbecue sauce

2 teaspoons fresh grated ginger

1 cup chopped fresh mango (about 1 medium mango)

2 tablespoons finely chopped red onion

1 tablespoon chopped fresh cilantro

1 tablespoon finely chopped seeded jalapeño pepper*

2 teaspoons lime juice

Jalapeño peppers can sting and irritate the skin, so wear rubber gloves when handling peppers and do not touch your eyes.

1 Soak four wooden skewers in water 20 minutes. Cook rice according to package directions; set aside.

2 Prepare grill for direct cooking. Oil grid.

3 Thread shrimp onto skewers, leaving ⅛-inch space between shrimp. Combine barbecue sauce and ginger in small bowl; mix well.

4 Grill skewers over medium heat 6 to 7 minutes or until shrimp are pink and opaque, turning once and brushing frequently with barbecue sauce mixture.

5 Stir mango, onion, cilantro, jalapeño and lime juice into hot rice. Serve shrimp over rice mixture.

GRILLED SWORDFISH SICILIAN STYLE
MAKES 4 TO 6 SERVINGS

3 tablespoons extra virgin olive oil

1 clove garlic, minced

2 tablespoons lemon juice

¾ teaspoon salt

⅛ teaspoon black pepper

3 tablespoons capers, drained

1 tablespoon chopped fresh oregano or basil

1½ pounds swordfish steaks, ¾ inch thick

1 Prepare grill for direct cooking. Oil grid.

2 Heat oil in small saucepan over low heat. Add garlic; cook and stir 1 minute. Remove from heat; cool slightly. Stir in lemon juice, salt and pepper until well blended. Stir in capers and oregano.

3 Grill swordfish over medium heat 7 to 8 minutes or until center is opaque, turning once. Top with sauce.

VARIATION

The garlic and lemon sauce can also be used as a marinade for the fish instead of a sauce after grilling.

FISH TACOS WITH YOGURT SAUCE
MAKES 6 SERVINGS

SAUCE

½ cup plain yogurt

¼ cup chopped fresh cilantro

3 tablespoons sour cream

Juice of 1 lime

1 tablespoon mayonnaise

½ teaspoon ground cumin

¼ teaspoon ground red pepper

Salt and black pepper

TACOS

Juice of ½ lime

2 tablespoons canola oil

1½ pounds swordfish, halibut or tilapia fillets

Salt and ground black pepper

12 corn or flour tortillas

3 cups shredded cabbage or prepared coleslaw

2 medium tomatoes, chopped

1 Combine yogurt, cilantro, sour cream, juice of 1 lime, mayonnaise, cumin and red pepper in small bowl; mix well. Season with salt and black pepper.

2 Prepare grill for direct cooking. Oil grid.

3 Combine juice of ½ lime and oil in small bowl; brush mixture over swordfish about 5 minutes before cooking. Season with salt and black pepper. (Do not marinate fish longer than about 5 minutes, or acid in lime juice will begin to "cook" fish.)

4 Grill swordfish, covered, over high heat 5 minutes per side or until center is opaque. Remove to plate; break into large pieces.

5 Grill tortillas 10 seconds per side or until beginning to bubble and brown lightly. Fill tortillas with fish; top with sauce, cabbage and tomatoes.

TERIYAKI SHRIMP AND MANGO KABOBS OVER ORZO
MAKES 4 SERVINGS

10 ounces large raw shrimp (21 to 25 per pound), peeled and deveined (with tails on)

¼ cup reduced-sodium teriyaki sauce

14 cherry tomatoes, divided

1½ cups reduced-sodium chicken broth

1 cup uncooked orzo pasta

½ cup water

1 clove garlic, minced

4 cups baby spinach

½ teaspoon black pepper

9 green onions, trimmed and cut into 2-inch pieces

1 mango, cut into 1½-inch pieces

1 Place shrimp in large resealable food storage bag. Pour teriyaki sauce over shrimp. Seal bag; turn to coat. Marinate in refrigerator at least 1 hour.

2 Meanwhile, chop 6 cherry tomatoes; set aside. Combine broth, orzo, water and garlic in large saucepan; bring to a boil over high heat. Reduce heat to medium-low; cover and cook 10 minutes. Stir in spinach, chopped tomatoes and pepper; cook 2 to 3 minutes until spinach is wilted and orzo is tender.

3 Soak four wooden skewers in water 20 minutes. Prepare grill for direct cooking.

4 Remove shrimp from teriyaki sauce; reserve teriyaki sauce. Alternately thread shrimp, remaining 8 cherry tomatoes, green onions and mango onto skewers. Brush both sides of skewers with reserved teriyaki sauce.

5 Grill skewers over medium-high heat 6 to 8 minutes or until shrimp are pink and opaque, turning once. Serve over orzo.

GRILLED SALMON, ASPARAGUS AND ONIONS
MAKES 6 SERVINGS

6 salmon fillets (6 to 8 ounces each)

½ teaspoon paprika

⅓ cup prepared honey-Dijon marinade or barbecue sauce

1 pound fresh asparagus spears, ends trimmed

1 large red or sweet onion, cut into ¼-inch slices

1 tablespoon olive oil

Salt and black pepper

1 Prepare grill for direct grilling. Oil grid. Sprinkle both sides of salmon with paprika; brush with marinade. Let stand at room temperature 15 minutes.

2 Brush asparagus and onion slices with oil; season with salt and pepper.

3 Place salmon, skin side down, in center of grid. Place asparagus and onion slices around salmon. Grill, covered, over medium heat 5 minutes. Turn salmon and vegetables; grill 5 to 6 minutes or until fish begins to flake when tested with fork and vegetables are crisp-tender. Separate onion slices into rings; serve over asparagus.

GRILLED TILAPIA WITH ZESTY MUSTARD SAUCE
MAKES 4 SERVINGS

2 tablespoons butter, softened

1 teaspoon Dijon mustard

½ teaspoon grated lemon peel

½ teaspoon Worcestershire sauce

½ teaspoon salt, divided

¼ teaspoon black pepper

4 tilapia fillets (about 4 ounces each)

1½ teaspoons paprika

½ lemon, quartered

2 tablespoons minced fresh parsley (optional)

1 Prepare grill for direct cooking. Oil grid or grill basket.

2 Combine butter, mustard, lemon peel, Worcestershire sauce, ¼ teaspoon salt and pepper in small bowl; mix well.

3 Rinse tilapia; pat dry with paper towels. Sprinkle both sides of tilapia with paprika and remaining ¼ teaspoon salt.

4 Grill tilapia, covered, over high heat 3 minutes. Turn and grill, covered, 2 to 3 minutes or until fish begins to flake when tested with fork.

5 Squeeze one lemon wedge over each fillet. Spread butter mixture over tilapia; sprinkle with parsley, if desired.

GRILLED HALIBUT WITH CHERRY TOMATO RELISH
MAKES 4 SERVINGS

4 halibut fillets (about 6 ounces each)
3 tablespoons lemon juice, divided
2 tablespoons olive oil, divided
2 teaspoons grated lemon peel, divided
2 cloves garlic, minced
½ teaspoon salt, divided
½ teaspoon black pepper, divided
2 cups cherry tomatoes, quartered
2 tablespoons chopped fresh parsley

1 Place halibut in large resealable food storage bag. Combine 2 tablespoons lemon juice, 1 tablespoon oil, 1 teaspoon lemon peel, garlic, ¼ teaspoon salt and ¼ teaspoon pepper in small bowl; pour over halibut. Seal bag; turn to coat. Marinate in refrigerator 1 hour.

2 Combine tomatoes, parsley, remaining 1 tablespoon lemon juice, 1 tablespoon oil, 1 teaspoon lemon peel, ¼ teaspoon salt and ¼ teaspoon pepper in medium bowl; mix well.

3 Prepare grill for direct cooking. Oil grid. Remove halibut from marinade; discard marinade.

4 Grill halibut over medium-high heat 3 to 5 minutes per side or until fish begins to flake when tested with fork. Serve with relish.

GRILLED BAJA BURRITOS
MAKES 4 SERVINGS

 1 pound tilapia fillets
 4 tablespoons vegetable oil, divided
 3 tablespoons lime juice, divided
 2 teaspoons chili powder
1½ teaspoons lemon-pepper seasoning
 3 cups coleslaw mix
½ cup chopped fresh cilantro
¼ teaspoon salt
¼ teaspoon black pepper
 Guacamole and pico de gallo (optional)
 4 (7-inch) flour tortillas
 Lime wedges (optional)

1 Prepare grill for direct cooking. Oil grid.

2 Place tilapia in large resealable food storage bag. Combine 2 tablespoons oil, 1 tablespoon lime juice, chili powder and lemon-pepper seasoning in small bowl; pour over tilapia. Seal bag; turn to coat. Let stand at room temperature 10 minutes.

3 Combine coleslaw mix, remaining 2 tablespoons oil, 2 tablespoons lime juice, cilantro, salt and pepper in medium bowl; mix well. Remove tilapia from marinade; discard marinade.

4 Grill tilapia, covered, over medium-high heat 3 to 4 minutes per side or until center is opaque. Remove to plate; break into large pieces.

5 Layer tilapia, coleslaw mixture, guacamole and pico de gallo, if desired, on tortillas; roll up tightly into burritos. Serve with additional pico de gallo and lime wedges, if desired.

TIP
Any firm white fish, such as snapper or halibut,
can be substitute for the tilapia.

CEDAR PLANK SALMON WITH GRILLED CITRUS MANGO
MAKES 4 SERVINGS

4 salmon fillets (6 ounces each), skin intact

2 teaspoons sugar, divided

1 teaspoon chili powder

½ teaspoon black pepper

¼ teaspoon salt

¼ teaspoon ground allspice

2 tablespoons orange juice

1 tablespoon lemon juice

1 tablespoon lime juice

2 teaspoons minced fresh ginger

¼ cup chopped fresh mint

⅛ teaspoon red pepper flakes

2 medium mangos, peeled and cut into 1-inch pieces

1 cedar plank (about 15×7 inches, ½ inch thick), soaked*

*Soak in water 5 hours or overnight.

1 Soak wooden skewers in water 20 minutes. Prepare grill for direct cooking.

2 Rinse salmon and pat dry. Combine 1 teaspoon sugar, chili powder, black pepper, salt and allspice in small bowl; mix well. Rub over flesh side of fish.

3 Combine remaining 1 teaspoon sugar, orange juice, lemon juice, lime juice, ginger, mint and red pepper flakes in medium bowl; mix well.

4 Thread mango pieces onto skewers or spread out in grill basket.

5 Turn heat on gas grill down to medium. Keep clean spray bottle filled with water nearby in case plank begins to burn. If it flares up, spray lightly with water. Lightly brush grid with oil and place soaked plank on top. Cover grill and heat until plank smokes and crackles.

6 Place salmon, skin side down, on plank and arrange mango skewers alongside plank. Grill, covered, over medium-high heat 6 to 8 minutes or until mango pieces are slightly charred, turning skewers frequently. Remove mango from grill. Grill salmon, covered, 9 to 12 minutes or until fish begins to flake when tested with fork.

7 Remove plank from grill; transfer salmon to serving platter. Slide mango pieces off skewers and add to mint mixture; toss gently to coat. Serve immediately with salmon.

TIP

Cedar planks can be purchased at gourmet kitchen stores or hardware stores. Be sure to buy untreated wood at least ½ inch thick. Use each plank for grilling food only once. Used planks may be broken up into wood chips and used to smoke foods.

VEGETABLES & SIDES

CHILI-RUBBED GRILLED VEGETABLE KABOBS

MAKES 4 SERVINGS

2 ears corn, husked and cut into 1-inch pieces

1 red bell pepper, cut into 12 (1-inch) pieces

1 yellow bell pepper, cut into 12 (1-inch) pieces

1 green bell pepper, cut into 12 (1-inch) pieces

1 medium sweet or red onion, cut into 12 wedges

2 tablespoons olive oil

1 teaspoon seasoned salt

1 teaspoon chili powder

½ teaspoon sugar

1 Alternately thread corn, bell peppers and onion onto 12-inch metal skewers. Brush oil over vegetables.

2 Combine seasoned salt, chili powder and sugar in small bowl; mix well. Sprinkle over all sides of vegetables. Wrap skewers in heavy-duty foil; refrigerate up to 8 hours.

3 Prepare grill for direct cooking.

4 Grill skewers (unwrapped) over medium heat 10 to 12 minutes or until vegetables are tender, turning occasionally.

GRILLED POTATO SALAD

MAKES 4 SERVINGS

¼ cup country-style Dijon mustard

2 tablespoons chopped fresh dill

1 tablespoon white wine vinegar or cider vinegar

1½ teaspoons salt, divided

¼ teaspoon black pepper

5 tablespoons olive oil, divided

8 cups water

2 pounds small red potatoes, cut into ½-inch slices

1 green onion, thinly sliced

1 Combine mustard, dill, vinegar, ½ teaspoon salt and pepper in small bowl; mix well. Gradually whisk in 3 tablespoons oil until blended. Set aside.

2 Prepare grill for direct cooking.

3 Bring water and remaining 1 teaspoon salt to a boil in large saucepan over medium-high heat. Add potatoes; boil 5 minutes. Drain and return potatoes to saucepan. Drizzle with remaining 2 tablespoons oil; toss gently to coat.

4 Spray one side of large foil sheet with nonstick cooking spray. Transfer potatoes to foil; fold into packet.

5 Grill packet 10 minutes or until potatoes are tender. Transfer potatoes to serving bowl. Add dressing and green onion; toss gently to coat. Serve warm.

GEMELLI AND GRILLED SUMMER VEGETABLES
MAKES 4 SERVINGS

2 large bell peppers (red and yellow), halved and seeded

12 stalks asparagus, trimmed

2 slices red onion

3 tablespoons plus 1 teaspoon olive oil, divided

6 ounces (2¼ cups) uncooked gemelli or rotini pasta

2 tablespoons pine nuts

1 clove garlic

1 cup loosely packed fresh basil leaves

¼ cup grated Parmesan cheese

¼ teaspoon salt

¼ teaspoon black pepper

1 cup grape or cherry tomatoes

1 Prepare grill for direct cooking. Grill bell peppers, skin side down, covered, over medium-high heat 10 to 12 minutes or until skins are blackened. Transfer peppers to paper bag; close bag and let stand 10 to 15 minutes. Remove charred skins. Cut peppers into 1-inch pieces; place in large bowl.

2 Brush asparagus and onion with 1 teaspoon oil. Grill, covered, over medium heat 8 to 10 minutes or until tender, turning once. Cut asparagus into 2-inch pieces and coarsely chop onion; add to bowl with peppers.

3 Cook pasta according to package directions; drain well and add to vegetables.

4 Combine pine nuts and garlic in food processor; process until coarsely chopped. Add basil; process until finely chopped. With motor running, add remaining 3 tablespoons oil; process until blended. Stir in Parmesan, salt and black pepper. Add basil mixture and tomatoes to pasta and vegetables; toss gently to coat. Serve immediately.

GRILLED VEGETABLE PIZZAS

MAKES 4 MAIN-DISH OR 8 APPETIZER SERVINGS

2 tablespoons olive oil

1 clove garlic, minced

1 red bell pepper, cut into quarters

4 slices red onion (¼-inch slices)

1 medium zucchini, halved lengthwise

1 medium yellow squash, halved lengthwise

1 cup prepared pizza sauce

¼ teaspoon red pepper flakes

2 (10-inch) prepared pizza crusts

2 cups (8 ounces) shredded fontinella or mozzarella cheese

¼ cup sliced fresh basil

1 Prepare grill for direct cooking.

2 Combine oil and garlic in small bowl; brush over bell pepper, onion, zucchini and yellow squash.

3 Grill vegetables, covered, over medium heat 10 minutes or until crisp-tender, turning once.

4 Cut bell pepper lengthwise into ¼-inch strips. Cut zucchini and squash crosswise into ¼-inch slices. Separate onion slices into rings.

5 Combine pizza sauce and red pepper flakes in small bowl; spread over pizza crusts. Top with cheese and grilled vegetables.

6 Grill pizzas, covered, over medium-low heat 5 to 6 minutes or until crust is hot and cheese is melted. Sprinkle with basil.

GRILLED TRI-COLORED PEPPER SALAD
MAKES 4 TO 6 SERVINGS

1 *each* large red, yellow and green bell pepper, cut into halves or quarters and seeded

⅓ cup extra virgin olive oil

3 tablespoons balsamic vinegar

2 cloves garlic, minced

½ teaspoon salt

¼ teaspoon black pepper

½ cup crumbled goat cheese

¼ cup thinly sliced fresh basil

1 Prepare grill for direct cooking.

2 Grill bell peppers, skin side down, covered, over medium-high heat 10 to 12 minutes or until skins are blackened. Transfer peppers to paper bag; close bag and let stand 10 to 15 minutes. Remove charred skins. Place bell peppers in shallow serving dish.

3 Combine oil, vinegar, garlic, salt and black pepper in small bowl; mix well. Pour over bell peppers; turn to coat. Let stand at room temperature 30 minutes. (Or cover and refrigerate up to 24 hours. Bring peppers to room temperature before serving.)

4 Sprinkle with goat cheese and basil just before serving.

GRILLED FRUITS WITH ORANGE COUSCOUS

MAKES 4 SERVINGS

1⅓ cups quick-cooking couscous

½ teaspoon ground cinnamon

½ cup orange juice

2 tablespoons vegetable oil, divided

1 tablespoon soy sauce

1 tablespoon maple syrup

⅛ teaspoon ground nutmeg

½ cup raisins

½ cup chopped walnuts or pecans

2 ripe mangoes, quartered

½ medium pineapple, cut into ½-inch slices

1 Prepare grill for direct cooking. Oil grid.

2 Prepare couscous according to package directions, adding cinnamon to water with couscous.

3 Meanwhile, combine orange juice, 1 tablespoon oil, soy sauce and maple syrup in small bowl; mix well. Combine remaining 1 tablespoon oil and nutmeg in small cup; set aside.

4 Cool couscous 5 minutes. Stir in orange juice mixture, raisins and walnuts until blended. Cover loosely to keep warm.

5 Place mangoes, skin side down, and pineapple on grid; brush with nutmeg mixture. Grill over medium-high heat 5 to 7 minutes or until fruits soften, turning pineapple once. Serve fruits with couscous.

MEXICAN-STYLE CORN ON THE COB ▶
MAKES 4 SERVINGS

2 tablespoons mayonnaise

½ teaspoon chili powder

½ teaspoon grated lime peel

4 ears corn, shucked

2 tablespoons grated Parmesan cheese

1 Prepare grill for direct cooking. Combine mayonnaise, chili powder and lime peel in small bowl; mix well.

2 Grill corn over medium-high heat 4 to 6 minutes or until lightly charred, turning 3 times. Immediately spread mayonnaise mixture over corn. Sprinkle with Parmesan.

GRILLED SESAME ASPARAGUS
MAKES 4 SERVINGS

1 pound medium asparagus spears (about 20), trimmed

1 tablespoon sesame seeds

2 teaspoons vegetable oil

2 to 3 teaspoons balsamic vinegar

¼ teaspoon salt

¼ teaspoon black pepper

1 Prepare grill for direct cooking. Oil grid.

2 Combine asparagus, sesame seeds and oil in large bowl or on baking sheet; toss to coat.

3 Grill asparagus over medium-high heat 4 to 6 minutes or until beginning to brown, turning once.

4 Sprinkle with vinegar, salt and pepper. Serve warm or at room temperature.

VEGETABLES & SIDES

GRILLED BEET SALAD
MAKES 4 SERVINGS

6 medium red beets (about 1½ pounds), peeled and cut into 1-inch pieces

1 medium yellow onion, cut into ½-inch wedges

8 ounces carrots, halved lengthwise and cut into 1-inch pieces

¼ cup plus 2 tablespoons olive oil, divided

3 tablespoons balsamic vinegar

1 clove garlic, minced

½ teaspoon salt

½ teaspoon dried rosemary

¼ teaspoon black pepper

6 cups chopped spring greens (two 5-ounce packages)

1 cup pecan pieces, toasted* or candied pecans

½ cup Gorgonzola or goat cheese, crumbled

*To toast pecans, cook in heavy medium skillet over medium heat 1 to 2 minutes or until lightly browned, stirring frequently. Immediately remove from skillet; cool before using.

1 Prepare grill for direct cooking.

2 Place beets in microwavable dish; cover and microwave on HIGH 6 to 8 minutes or until slightly soft. Cool to room temperature; pat dry with paper towels.

3 Divide beets, onion and carrots evenly between two 12×8-inch disposable foil pans. Drizzle 1 tablespoon oil over vegetables in each pan; toss to coat. Arrange vegetables in single layer. Cover pans loosely with foil.

4 Place pans on grid. Grill over medium-high heat 22 to 25 minutes or until fork-tender, stirring every 5 minutes. Cool completely.

5 Combine remaining ¼ cup oil, vinegar, garlic, salt, rosemary and pepper in small bowl; mix well.

6 Place greens in serving bowl or on platter. Add half of vinaigrette; toss gently. Top with grilled vegetables; drizzle with remaining vinaigrette. Top with pecans and cheese. Serve immediately.

TIP

To peel beets, trim ends, then peel with a vegetable peeler under running water to help minimize the beet juice staining your hands.

SZECHUAN GRILLED MUSHROOMS
MAKES 4 SERVINGS

1 pound large mushrooms

2 tablespoons soy sauce

2 teaspoons peanut or vegetable oil

1 teaspoon dark sesame oil

1 clove garlic, minced

½ teaspoon crushed Szechuan peppercorns or red pepper flakes

1 Place mushrooms in large resealable food storage bag. Combine soy sauce, peanut oil, sesame oil, garlic and Szechuan peppercorns in small bowl; pour over mushrooms. Seal bag; turn to coat. Marinate at room temperature 15 minutes.

2 Soak wooden skewers in water 20 minutes. Prepare grill for direct cooking. Thread mushrooms onto skewers.

3 Grill mushrooms over medium heat 10 minutes or until lightly browned, turning once. Serve immediately.

VARIATION

Add 4 green onions, cut into 1½-inch pieces, to the marinade. Alternately thread the green onions onto the skewers with the mushrooms. Grill as directed.

SPAGHETTI SQUASH WITH BLACK BEANS AND ZUCCHINI
MAKES 4 SERVINGS

1 spaghetti squash (about 2 pounds)

2 medium zucchini, cut lengthwise into ¼-inch-thick slices

2 tablespoons plus 1 teaspoon olive oil, divided

2 cups chopped seeded fresh tomatoes

1 can (about 15 ounces) black beans, rinsed and drained

2 tablespoons chopped fresh basil

2 tablespoons red wine vinegar

1 clove garlic, minced

½ teaspoon salt

1 Prepare grill for direct cooking. Pierce spaghetti squash in several places with fork. Place in center of large piece of heavy-duty foil. Bring two long sides of foil together above squash; fold down in series of locked folds, allowing room for heat circulation and expansion. Fold short ends up and over again. Press folds firmly to seal foil packet.

2 Grill squash, covered, over medium heat 45 minutes to 1 hour or until easily depressed with back of long-handled spoon, turning one quarter turn every 15 minutes. Remove squash from grill; let stand in foil 10 to 15 minutes.

3 Meanwhile, brush both sides of zucchini slices with 1 teaspoon oil. Grill, uncovered, over medium heat 4 minutes or until tender, turning once. Cut into bite-size pieces.

4 Remove spaghetti squash from foil; cut in half and remove seeds. Separate squash into strands with two forks; place on large serving plate.

5 Combine zucchini, tomatoes, beans and basil in medium bowl. Combine remaining 2 tablespoons oil, vinegar, garlic and salt in small bowl; mix well. Add to vegetables; toss gently to coat. Serve over spaghetti squash.

GRILLED STONE FRUIT SALAD
MAKES 4 SERVINGS

2 tablespoons orange juice

1 tablespoon lemon juice

2 teaspoons canola oil

1 teaspoon honey

½ teaspoon Dijon mustard

1 tablespoon finely chopped fresh mint

1 medium peach, halved and pitted

1 medium nectarine, halved and pitted

1 medium plum, halved and pitted

4 cups mixed baby greens

½ cup crumbled goat cheese

1 Prepare grill for direct cooking. Oil grid.

2 Combine orange juice, lemon juice, oil, honey and mustard in small bowl; mix well. Stir in mint. Brush dressing over cut sides of fruits; set remaining dressing aside.

3 Grill fruits, cut sides down, covered, over medium-high heat 2 to 3 minutes. Turn and grill 2 to 3 minutes or until fruits begin to soften. Remove to plate; let stand until cool enough to handle. Cut into wedges.

4 Divide mixed greens among four serving plates; top with fruits and goat cheese. Drizzle with remaining dressing. Serve immediately.

JAMAICAN GRILLED SWEET POTATOES
MAKES 6 SERVINGS

2 large sweet potatoes (about 1½ pounds)

3 tablespoons packed brown sugar

3 tablespoons butter, melted, divided

1 teaspoon ground ginger

1 tablespoon chopped fresh cilantro

2 teaspoons dark rum

1 Pierce sweet potatoes in several places with fork. Place on paper towel in microwave. Microwave on HIGH 5 to 6 minutes or until crisp-tender, rotating one quarter turn halfway through cooking time. Let stand 10 minutes. Cut sweet potatoes diagonally into ¾-inch slices.

2 Prepare grill for direct cooking.

3 Combine brown sugar, 1 tablespoon butter and ginger in small bowl; mix well. Stir in cilantro and rum.

4 Lightly brush one side of each sweet potato slice with half of remaining butter.

5 Grill sweet potato slices, butter side down, covered, over medium heat 4 to 6 minutes or until grillmarked. Brush with remaining butter; turn and grill 3 to 5 minutes or until grillmarked. Remove to serving platter; drizzle with rum mixture.

ITALIAN VEGETARIAN GRILL
MAKES 4 TO 6 SERVINGS

4 large bell peppers, quartered

4 medium zucchini, cut lengthwise into ½-inch slices

1 pound asparagus (about 20 spears), trimmed

2 large red onions, cut into ½-inch slices

½ cup olive oil

2 teaspoons salt, divided

1 teaspoon Italian seasoning

1 teaspoon black pepper, divided

4 cups water

1 cup uncooked polenta

4 ounces crumbled goat cheese

1 Arrange bell peppers, zucchini and asparagus in single layer on two baking sheets. To hold onion together securely, pierce slices horizontally with metal skewers. Add to baking sheet. Combine oil, 1 teaspoon salt, Italian seasoning and ½ teaspoon black pepper in small bowl. Brush mixture generously over vegetables, turning to coat all sides.

2 Prepare grill for direct cooking. Meanwhile, bring water and remaining 1 teaspoon salt to a boil in large saucepan over high heat. Gradually whisk in polenta. Reduce heat to medium; cook until polenta thickens and begins to pull away from side of pan, stirring constantly. Stir in remaining ½ teaspoon black pepper. Keep warm.

3 Grill vegetables, covered, over medium-high heat 10 to 15 minutes or until tender, turning once. Place bell peppers in large bowl or paper bag; cover and let stand 10 minutes. Remove charred skins. Cut all vegetables into bite-size pieces.

4 Spoon polenta into bowls; top with vegetables and goat cheese.

NAAN (INDIAN FLATBREAD)
MAKES 12 SERVINGS

1 packet (¼ ounce) active dry yeast

1 teaspoon sugar

¼ cup plus 2 tablespoons warm water, divided

3 cups all-purpose flour

1 teaspoon salt

1 teaspoon kalonji* seeds or poppy seeds (optional)

½ cup plain whole milk Greek yogurt

¼ cup (½ stick) melted butter, plus additional butter for brushing on naan

Kalonji seed is often called onion seed or black cumin seed. It is available in Indian markets and is traditional in some varieties of naan.

1 Stir yeast and sugar into 2 tablespoons water in small bowl; let stand 10 minutes or until foamy. Combine flour, salt and kalonji, if desired, in bowl of stand mixer. Attach dough hook; stir until blended.

2 Add yeast mixture, yogurt and ¼ cup butter; mix at low speed until combined. Add remaining ¼ cup water by tablespoonfuls, mixing at low speed until dough comes together and cleans side of bowl. (You may not need all the water.) Knead at low speed 5 to 7 minutes or until dough is smooth and elastic.

3 Shape dough into a ball. Place in greased bowl; turn to grease top. Cover and let rise in warm place 1½ to 2 hours or until doubled in size.

4 Punch dough down; divide into six pieces. Roll into balls and place on plate sprayed with nonstick cooking spray. Cover and let rest 10 to 15 minutes.

5 Meanwhile, prepare grill for direct cooking. Place each ball of dough on lightly floured surface; roll and stretch into ⅛-inch-thick oval.

6 Place dough pieces on grid two or three at a time. Grill, covered, over high heat 2 minutes or until puffed. Turn and brush tops with butter; grill 1 to 2 minutes or until browned in patches on both sides. Brush bottoms with additional butter; serve warm.

METRIC CONVERSION CHART

VOLUME MEASUREMENTS (dry)

1/8 teaspoon = 0.5 mL
1/4 teaspoon = 1 mL
1/2 teaspoon = 2 mL
3/4 teaspoon = 4 mL
1 teaspoon = 5 mL
1 tablespoon = 15 mL
2 tablespoons = 30 mL
1/4 cup = 60 mL
1/3 cup = 75 mL
1/2 cup = 125 mL
2/3 cup = 150 mL
3/4 cup = 175 mL
1 cup = 250 mL
2 cups = 1 pint = 500 mL
3 cups = 750 mL
4 cups = 1 quart = 1 L

VOLUME MEASUREMENTS (fluid)

1 fluid ounce (2 tablespoons) = 30 mL
4 fluid ounces (1/2 cup) = 125 mL
8 fluid ounces (1 cup) = 250 mL
12 fluid ounces (1 1/2 cups) = 375 mL
16 fluid ounces (2 cups) = 500 mL

WEIGHTS (mass)

1/2 ounce = 15 g
1 ounce = 30 g
3 ounces = 90 g
4 ounces = 120 g
8 ounces = 225 g
10 ounces = 285 g
12 ounces = 360 g
16 ounces = 1 pound = 450 g

DIMENSIONS

1/16 inch = 2 mm
1/8 inch = 3 mm
1/4 inch = 6 mm
1/2 inch = 1.5 cm
3/4 inch = 2 cm
1 inch = 2.5 cm

OVEN TEMPERATURES

250°F = 120°C
275°F = 140°C
300°F = 150°C
325°F = 160°C
350°F = 180°C
375°F = 190°C
400°F = 200°C
425°F = 220°C
450°F = 230°C

BAKING PAN SIZES

Utensil	Size in Inches/Quarts	Metric Volume	Size in Centimeters
Baking or Cake Pan (square or rectangular)	8×8×2	2 L	20×20×5
	9×9×2	2.5 L	23×23×5
	12×8×2	3 L	30×20×5
	13×9×2	3.5 L	33×23×5
Loaf Pan	8×4×3	1.5 L	20×10×7
	9×5×3	2 L	23×13×7
Round Layer Cake Pan	8×1½	1.2 L	20×4
	9×1½	1.5 L	23×4
Pie Plate	8×1¼	750 mL	20×3
	9×1¼	1 L	23×3
Baking Dish or Casserole	1 quart	1 L	—
	1½ quart	1.5 L	—
	2 quart	2 L	—